Lost Souls: FOUND!™

Inspiring Stories About Boxers

Kyla Duffy and Lowrey Mumford

Published by Happy Tails Books™, LLC

Happy Tails Books™ (HTB) uses the power of storytelling to effect positive changes in the lives of animals in need. The joy, hope, and (occasional) chaos these stories describe will make you laugh and cry, as you em*bark* on a journey with these authors who are guardians and/or fosters of adopted dogs. "Reading for Rescue" with HTB not only brings further awareness to rescue efforts and breed characteristics, but each sale also results in a financial contribution to dog rescue groups.

Lost Souls: Found!™ Inspiring Stories About Boxers by Kyla Duffy and Lowrey Mumford

Published by Happy Tails Books™, LLC www.happytailsbooks.com

The publisher gratefully acknowledges the numerous Boxer rescue groups and their members, who generously granted permission to use their stories and photos.

The following brand names mentioned in this book are registered trademarks and the property of their owners. The author and publishing company make no claims to the logos mentioned in this book including: Petsmart, Jeep, McDonald's, Craigslist, Dr's Foster and Smith, Gorilla Tough, Prozac

Photo Credits (All Rights Reserved by Photographers):

Front Cover: Allie, Kelly Dunn, www.justimagineinc.com
Back Cover Top: Titan, Abbie Cooke, chariotcreative.com
Back Cover L: Jezabel, Whitney Price
Back Cover Mid: Alice, April Turner, uturnstudios.com
Back Cover R: Bruin and Ruger, Abbie Cooke
Inside Title: Beau and Nike, Kelly Dunn
P10: Grace, Abbie Cooke

Publishers Cataloging In Publication

Lost Souls: Found!™ Inspiring Stories About Boxers/ [Compiled and edited by] Kyla Duffy and Lowrey Mumford.

p. ; cm.

ISBN: 978-0-9824895-3-6

1. Boxer Dogs. 2. Dog rescue. 3. Dogs – Anecdotes. 4. Animal welfare – United States. 5. Human-animal relationships – Anecdotes. I. Duffy, Kyla. II. Mumford, Lowrey. III. Title.

SF426.5   2010

636.73   2010900021

Happy Tails Books appreciates all of the contributors and rescue groups whose thought-provoking stories make this book come to life. We'd like to send a special thanks to:

Blue Ridge Boxer Rescue
http://www.blueridgeboxerrescue.com/

Boxer Buddies
http://www.boxerbuddies.org/

Heart of Ohio Boxer Rescue
http://www.heartofohioboxerrescue.com/

Legacy Boxer Rescue
http://www.savetheboxers.com/

Mid Michigan Boxer Rescue
http://www.midmichiganboxerrescue.org/

Midwest Boxer Rescues
http://www.midwestboxerrescues.com/

Missouri Valley Boxer Club
http://www.mvboxerclub.com/

Mokan Boxer Rescue
http://www.petfinder.com/shelters/KS01.html

Norcal Boxer Rescue
http://www.ncbr.org/

Rockin' P Rescue
http://www.rockinprescue.org/

Want more info about the dogs, authors, and rescues featured in this book? http://happytailsbooks.com

Table of Contents

Introduction: The Revelation

Almost a decade ago I brought home a Boxer puppy for my husband. Damon always talked so fondly of his previous Boxer, Hammer, and I knew he longed to have another. He always said Hammer was smart but never warned me about Boxer puppyhood and adolescence. It appeared that while Hammer (new puppy, old name) was my husband's gift, I was the one in for a surprise!

To say Hammer was a handful is an understatement. He could go from sweet puppy to demon spawn in under ten seconds. He chewed up my furniture and destroyed the house, but what made me love this little pup so very much? More importantly, what had I gotten myself into?

I started researching the Boxer breed. I know, I seriously put the cart before the horse on that one, but better late than never, right? (I strongly encourage others to read about a breed *before* bringing a dog into their homes.) I joined blogs and discussion groups on Boxers to try and find out what made our little guy so "special." Much to my surprise, I learned that Hammer was a *typical* Boxer puppy! I also discovered that canine companionship might do him some good. At the time, I couldn't imagine having two Boxer *puppies*, so instead I looked into rescuing a more mature dog. I ended up adopting a two-year-old female named Ginger and eventually became a foster parent, too!

During the next 12 months, something remarkable happened, and I found a passion within myself I had never known. Month after month I was overjoyed with the opportunity to take sad, lonely Boxers from shelters into my warm, loving home as a step towards finding them forever families. As I learned about animal overpopulation (the latest estimate by American Humane is that about four million dogs are euthanized in shelters each year), backyard breeding (inexperienced breeders who don't properly screen their breeding dogs for health and temperament), and puppy mills (doggie "sweat shops") my passion for rescue burned even brighter. My eyes had been opened and I could no longer stand by and watch the suffering. So I vowed to make a difference, one Boxer at a time.

Hammer introduced me to Boxers' funny, silly, playful nature—they're the clowns of the dog community. Originally bred to work as guard dogs, their muscular build and intimidating look served them, but their jovial personalities were their downfall. Nevertheless, Boxers are completely devoted to their families—protecting their homes and loved ones—without being prone to aggression (quite the opposite, in fact). Boxers love life, and they love to be near their people. It is this trait that fuels the passion in me for this breed, and I can't help but wonder: How can a breed, so loving and loyal to their people, face such cruelty and betrayal by the hands of those who are supposed to care for them?

While really there is no answer, my solution was, in 2004, to join forces with three like-minded individuals in forming Legacy Boxer Rescue (LBR). Lori, Brandi, Nivasha, and I ("The Founding Four") all shared the sentiment that no Boxer should be alone, cold, and afraid in a shelter, and together we were determined to make a difference.

I am often asked how I can stand to do rescue. Isn't it sad? Doesn't it make you furious the way people abuse and neglect animals? Don't you get attached and then you have to give them up? The answer to all of these questions is, of course, yes. But on the other hand, how can I not do rescue? How can I stand by and watch these wonderful animals perish? The answer is simple: I cannot.

LBR, like many of the other rescues who helped put this book together, was formed with the understanding that we would do our best to help all Boxers, regardless of age, infirmity, or known health problems. We knew we could not possibly save them all, but if we did our best, many would live good, full lives because of our efforts. Today, almost six years later, LBR has over 200 active volunteers in North Texas, and we have saved over 1,500 Boxers from certain death or worse.

Sadly, the task of rescuing Boxers has not lessened over time. Their rising popularity over the years has opened the door for unscrupulous backyard breeders and puppy millers to make a lot of money off of them. These breeders have no problem passing their dogs on to whoever is willing to pay, which is how many dogs end up in abusive situations and eventually get dumped in shelters. As long as there is money in dog breeding, overpopulation, abuse, and neglect will continue.

The stories herein will make you laugh and some will make you cry, but they all tell the "tail" of this wonderful breed and the people who love them. When you get to the end, don't worry if you feel a little different; it just means that Boxers have worked their way into your heart and soul, just like they did for me!

If you feel moved to do more to help Boxers, I hope you'll consider supporting your local shelter or rescue. Whether it is money or time you can contribute, your help is needed and appreciated. The very first step is to simply vow to make a difference; from there your heart will lead you. Enjoy...

 Sharon Sleighter, President, Legacy Boxer Rescue

Inspiring Stories
About Boxers

Love Goes Bonk

The day Abner made his way into my heart started out like any other weekend morning with grocery shopping, house cleaning, and surfing the Internet. We weren't actively searching for another dog, but on this particular day, I decided to look. Scrolling down the pages of the Midwest Boxer Rescue website, I stopped at a picture of a fawn Boxer who appeared to be winking at me. How odd... dogs can wink? As I scanned the latest update, the words, "I am blind," caused me to take a second look. Continuing on, my heart stopped at the sentence, "You would think that as cute as I am someone would have scooped me up, but everyone is afraid of me because I am blind." I knew right then that this was the dog we were going to adopt, regardless of the fact that we hadn't even discussed getting another dog yet.

I immediately went to my husband and said, "What do you think about looking for a playmate for Brooke-Lynn?" (Brooke-Lynn is our other Boxer.)

He said, "Sure, we can start looking."

Biting my lip, I said, "Don't be mad, but I think I already found one." I showed him Abner's story, and he agreed we were ready to handle the added responsibility and cost of another Boxer. Neither of us had ever had an animal with a handicap before, but we thought we could care for Abner. We were at least willing to try when so many others were not. I immediately started filling out the application so that we could (hopefully) adopt him.

Over the next few weeks, we learned that Abner was found in very poor condition: severely underweight, scratched up, and partially blind. Due to lack of space at the shelter, he had been stuffed in a kennel with a much larger, food-aggressive dog, who regularly attacked Abner. Nobody was sure whether the attacks by the larger dog or his prior abuse had led to his blindness, but, in any case, one of Abner's eyes had to be surgically removed, and the remaining one did not function at all. Despite all of these hardships, Abner was a sweet, friendly dog who wagged his little tail and did the Boxer "kidney bean" wiggle (the signature greeting of Boxers) every chance he got.

After several more emails with the rescue group, a very thorough home visit, and daily visits to Abner's web page, we were invited to visit Abner in Springfield, Missouri, which was a quick five hours away. About a week before we were scheduled to leave, a friend laughed when I told her I was cleaning up the house and moving all the chemicals to higher cabinets. "You're nesting!" she teased. I guess I was, because if everything worked out and everyone got along, we would be bringing Abner home with us that weekend.

After a looooong night in a hotel room with three kids and a scaredy-cat Boxer, who seemed to shake at every little noise or closing door, we were off to meet Abner and his foster family, the Frenches. We walked into the Frenches' house, and Abner greeted us in the living room. At only 40 pounds, he was much smaller than the 70-pound monster to which we were accustomed. He was quite friendly and playful with the human members of our family but was very defensive with Brooke-Lynn. It was clear he did not want a new dog in his house. Seeing Abner act this way towards Brooke-Lynn was the first time I felt doubt about this adoption. I mean, if the dogs didn't get along, would they even let us bring Abner home with us?

We decided to try the dogs on more neutral territory, so we took them to another foster family's home. This time Abner and Brooke-Lynn didn't quite hit it off, but they were at least tolerant of each other. I started to relax a little, and before we knew it, it was time for lunch and a final decision. We talked pros and cons over burgers and fries and decided to bring Abner into our family. (As if there was any doubt!) We went back to the Frenches' house, signed the paperwork, packed up Abner's things in our van, said our goodbyes, and set off for home. Abner made himself comfortable in the backseat with the kids and drifted off to sleep, while his "silly sounds" ball whooped, laughed, and roared whenever we hit a bump in the road.

After a nervous couple of hours driving through a horrible rain and lightning storm, we were home at last. The first order of business was walking Abner through the house so he could start to get his bearings. He bumped and nosed his way around for the rest of the evening and even tried to play with Brooke-Lynn a bit. It was rough at first while they figured out how each other played, resulting in some small nicks and unsure growls, but we could tell they were having fun getting to know each other.

My parents came to meet Abner the next day and were impressed at how quickly he had adapted to his new environment. Abner was already running in the backyard and maneuvering his way around the trees and fences, which led my dad to ask, "Are you sure he's completely blind?" As if he were listening and wanted to convince us, at just that moment, Abner ran right into the wall next to where my dad was standing, with a resounding "Bonk."

"Pretty sure..." I said, and we all laughed at Abner's timing. We lovingly referred to him as "Bonk" for the next couple of days.

Abner has been such a wonderful addition to our family, and he never ceases to amaze and impress us with his radiant spirit and gentle nature. We continue to learn new things about him even after all this time has gone by. He loves ice cubes but hates being wet. He loves peanut butter and will gently nibble while licking it off your finger. When he plays tag with Brooke-Lynn around the furniture, he can catch her even though she goes into stealth mode and doesn't make a sound. He can also catch a treat in mid-air when it's dropped in front of his nose. His favorite toy is a full-sized basketball, which he'll chase around the yard, barking at it for hours if we let him. Good luck getting it away from him; Abner protects it like it's a T-bone steak!

I once read that rescued animals were the best kinds of animals to adopt because they are so grateful to their new owners for taking them out of their horrible circumstances; Abner is living proof this sentiment is true. In his case, the dog who was severely underweight, abused, wounded, and disfigured has now become the happiest, sweetest, most well-adjusted dog imaginable. Our whole family is so appreciative of the rescue organization and Abner's foster family, the Frenches, for giving him a second chance at life...with us!

 *Meredith Thompson*

The Musical Queen

I t was nearly Thanksgiving when I was paging through the adoptable dogs on the Mid Michigan Boxer Rescue (MMBR) website and came across this delightful brindle Boxer girl named Yuki. She was the most wonderful-looking old lady—standing so proudly in her picture—with a pair of angel wings on her back. I said to my husband, "I want her!" and she became mine. (Okay, so I shared her with everyone.)

Yuki was found in the middle of a road after Labor Day. She was old with a huge, cancerous tumor on her neck, and someone had probably dumped her. After getting to know Yuki, we joke that we can actually picture her sitting there and saying, "Helloooo... I'm ready to be picked up now." She was so strong and independent but at the same time loving and fun.

The first day at our home we dubbed her "Yuki Gianna Francisco," and she just beamed and spun and spun. Hearing her full name must have given her such joy. She gave that joy right back to us by helping us create laughing memories we will never forget. For example, one day I came home and my husband, Todd, was laughing so hard he was crying. He told me about how he had heard a "wonderful musical scale" coming from the living room, even though nobody was home. Upon further investigation, Todd found Yuki sitting in the middle of the room with a look of ecstasy on her face, scratching her ear with her back paw and tooting a concerto fit for Mozart. The next day we were again blessed with a concert—what musical talent she possessed!

A few years back Yuki was crowned queen of the Mid Michigan Boxer Bash, a fitting title since she was already the queen of our home. The following year we returned to the bash, so Yuki could pass on her crown. On the way to the bash, Yuki shared her front seat with me and also shared my chocolate chip cookies. (She had decided she was my napkin, licking my lips after every bite, and nothing was going to stop her). The first person we saw at the bash was the king's mom, who also loved Yuki. Next Yuki greeted all of the volunteers and the directors. She was high-stepping and spinning with pride.

Unfortunately, after everyone had received their royal welcome, Yuki fell down with a seizure and passed away immediately. The cause of her death was a brain aneurism that had burst. Yuki seemed to have hung in there just to thank her "royal court" full of rescue friends and prance around as queen one last time before crossing the Rainbow Bridge.

We were devastated and couldn't even think about replacing her. I kept saying, "No new dogs. Never, never, never..."

But as the story always goes, it was only a few months later, just before Thanksgiving again, when my husband and I found another Boxer we needed to adopt. That's when "old man" MoElmer came into our lives.

MoElmer was apparently running free when he was caught and brought to a shelter. MMBR rescued him from that shelter and placed him in foster care. Since he was so old and thin, he was stuck there for a while. They didn't know if anyone would adopt him, but I think he was waiting for us! MMBR had named him Elmer, but he didn't look like an "Elmer" to us. We decided to change his name to Mo because "the Francisco's needed *mo'* Boxers in our lives." (Mo would be our fourth.)

The name "Mo" didn't last long because Todd decided "Mo" sounded too much like "No." Again on the name hunt, I decided to combine both names: "MoElmer John Francisco" became our new dog's formal name, but we kept calling him "Momo" for short.

Momo just needed weight and lots and lots of love, and we were more than happy to provide him with just that. His favorite hobbies turned out to be eating, sleeping, snacking, and napping, snoring with Mom on her bed, and occasionally letting out the loudest, smelliest toots in the world. Besides being loud and stinky, Momo is highly intelligent, well-trained, and incredibly laid back with no dominance issues.

We actually had to retrain him to lay on the couch with us. His hearing is not the greatest, he has no teeth, and he has cataracts, but boy does his sniffer work well. He can sniff out anything "peanut butter" with the best of them. He also has a huge capacity to love everyone, never knowing a stranger.

I never thought I could love another dog after Yuki, but since Momo came to us, I couldn't imagine life without him. He is truly a meat and potatoes kind of old man, and we are the luckiest people to have him in our lives.

 *Marie Francisco*

Tag... You're It!

This is a story not only of how I found a wonderful rescue dog, but how I found a calling of sorts and many lifelong friends. It was late February, and I was grieving from losing my big ole' Rottie, Rigger, to cancer. When he passed, he was about 13, which is pretty old for a Rottwieller. He'd had liver cancer for some time, so it wasn't an unexpected loss, but it hit me pretty hard. After a couple weeks of "being tough," I broke down and decided to look for a new furry friend.

As a veterinarian, I usually did not need to look hard for a dog, but at the time nobody had been abandoned or in need of a home at the clinic. I began pouring over Petfinder. com, looking for a male because my female Rottie didn't like girls on her turf. That narrowed my search, and then I remembered my old Boxer, Sparky. I adopted Sparky when his owner passed away, and even though he was ten and had cancer, he lived with me for another six great years. "Boxer it is," I thought, "preferably an older boy."

There were so many dogs needing homes on Petfinder, and I just kept looking and feeling disheartened. That is, until I came across Tag, this absolutely gorgeous male Boxer. (Tag, according to his write-up, means "handsome" in Irish.) Even though I was looking to adopt an older dog and this one was a puppy, I couldn't resist reading more. And then I saw it—Tag was listed as "donations only" to try and fund his medical care; he was *not* up for adoption. This six-month-old dog was apparently extremely sick, so sick that they expected he might die of a mystery illness.

I knew, almost at once, that this was the dog I needed to help. After all, I'm a veterinarian! Sure, the other vets were stumped, and maybe I would be too, but I knew I had to try. By this time I was so enamored with the young fellow that I printed his Petfinder photo out and showed it to my co-workers. I went to the rescue's website and sent them an email offering my help. After waiting almost a *whole hour* to hear back (I was anxious), I called the rescue, explained my situation, and asked if I could foster Tag or at least work on his medical problems.

Soon thereafter a woman called back and introduced herself as Beth, Tag's foster mommy. (I would later also come to know her as the director of the rescue.) Beth explained that Tag was always thirsty and urinated all the time, so his owners kept him in a garage, where they didn't care if he peed everywhere, before finally surrendering him to the rescue. He also had episodes where he seemed to be in terrible pain and wouldn't eat.

The rescue had spent thousands of dollars on vet visits and testing to no avail, so I asked Beth if they would mind me taking a look at him. She agreed and we arranged to meet at my office. I was doing a "happy dance," and apparently the board of directors of the rescue was, too! They shared with me later that they felt like they had won the lotto. Here was this veterinarian who was interested in the sickest dog they ever brought in, and she was calling *them* to see if she could help? Aside from perhaps Tag not being sick in the first place, the situation couldn't have been better.

About a week later, I met Tag. He came with an entourage; the director, her husband, the treasurer, and a couple volunteers all accompanied him to his appointment. Upon examining him I was even more smitten than when I first saw his picture. Tag was absolutely beautiful, fawn with a jet black muzzle and the most intense eyes I had ever seen. He was skinny because he spent most of his time drinking and peeing and often didn't want to eat. He peed twice in the office, but it didn't look intentional. He just couldn't help it. It was pathetic, but in spite of what he had been through, he wagged his stump and gave me a big Boxer kiss. My heart was melting right there in my chest. I arranged with the director for Tag to stay with me as my foster so I could further evaluate him.

The first week was very difficult for both Tag and me. I ran all the tests I could think of and still couldn't find any answers. He drank about five gallons of water a day and urinated every

15 minutes, even through the night. He had days of extreme pain, especially his neck, and he wouldn't eat or stand. By the second week I had ruled out some of the more common diseases that could have caused his symptoms.

It took another couple of weeks before I finally recognized his condition as a very rare, congenital disease found only in Boxers. Things improved dramatically once we had a diagnosis and began treatment, and after about a month and a half, Tag was finally on the road to recovery. He needed to have a very expensive medication three times a day, so I was lucky to be able to bring him to work with me. Since then he has gained about 10 pounds and all of his medical problems are completely controlled.

Naturally, I adopted Tag, and he goes everywhere with me. He motivated me to take him to obedience (twice) and even to try agility. He is my best friend, and he makes me smile, yet I feel like he's given me so much more than just friendship because he inspired me to become involved in rescue.

A month after adopting Tag, I decided to begin volunteering with Mid Michigan Boxer Rescue. This rescue does amazing things for dogs who would otherwise be abandoned and forgotten, and my experience with Tag showed me I could be of help. As a veterinarian for 23 years, I had worked with many other rescues, but this was the first time I felt truly needed and welcomed. Adopting Tag introduced me to an aspect of myself that I hadn't realized existed, and in the process I found some wonderful people, who are sure to be lifelong friends.

Joyce Heideman

The Little Ambassador

Alady and her husband were hiking in the desert one weekend when they noticed a small, white "something" running towards them from a great distance. As the *something* approached, they could see it was being chased by three coyotes. The white blur was only about fifteen feet away from being snatched when it reached the couple, who were now terrified, too. Nevertheless, instead of "throwing the dog to the wolves," they waved their arms and yelled, scaring the coyotes away. It was only then that they realized they had been protecting a young Boxer boy.

After taking him home, they named him Rocky and found out he was about eight months old. They couldn't keep him because they already had three dogs, so the woman brought Rocky to the local shelter. While describing her experience at work the next day, her co-workers (who knew a bit more than she did about the shelter) warned her that Rocky would most likely be put down. Being a kind-hearted person, she couldn't bear the thought of this poor dog having fought so hard for his life, only to be put down in a shelter, so she decided to again take action.

The woman went back to the shelter, paid the fee to take Rocky home, and called Boxer Luv Rescue, which is where I come in. I became involved with the rescue almost a year after losing my first Boxer to *cardiomyopathy* (a common, deadly heart condition). He was 10 and I was heartbroken, but working with a rescue organization helped pull me out of my grief.

The president of the rescue called one day and asked if I would be willing to foster a young, white, male Boxer who was found in the desert. I said yes and was in love the moment I met him. The first thing we did was visit the vet, who told me by the look of Rocky's foot pads, he had been in the desert for about a month. It was obvious Rocky had been thrown away, left out in the desert to die. His previous owners had cut his ears nearly off, and he was in pretty bad shape. Yet he survived.

I didn't foster Rocky. I instead took him home and adopted him for my own. Rocky was in heaven, and he quickly shared with us the special traits which most likely kept him alive while he was stray. Rocky regularly jumped up and picked oranges off the orange trees on our property. He was so smart that he would peel them and then take them inside to enjoy the "fruits" of his labor. He also could *chase down* birds in flight. Rocky would be lying on the back porch, and in an instant he would be after them like lightening, often catching birds before they even had a chance to take off.

Rocky didn't have a hard time assimilating into life as a "big brother" to our other foster dogs. He became known as "The Little Ambassador" because he was such a great big brother to the distressed dogs we regularly took in. He always welcomed each and every one and helped heal them in a way that only dogs can do for one another. He passed away from a brain tumor at the age of six-and-a-half, but during his more than five years with us, he was a great rescuer in his own right. In fact, Rocky was the embodiment of rescue: the love, patience, understanding, heartbreak, and all that goes with it.

I hope the people who rescued the little, white "something" from the desert that day know that their compassion didn't just save one life. Having the opportunity to get to know Rocky has had a lasting impact on many—both dogs and humans alike.

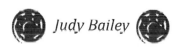 *Judy Bailey*

Love Moves Mountains... and Lifts Dogs

One of the most heart-wrenching experiences in my 30 years of doing rescue was also one of the most rewarding. I had ventured out on a rather dreary winter day to get some dog food and other small items, including bread and single-wrapped cheese, when my phone rang with a call from a woman who had a rescue emergency. She said she was from a construction company with office space in a large complex. When she arrived at work that day, she heard a noise under the deck and discovered a Boxer-looking dog huddled in the far back corner.

I arrived at the complex to find a crowd of onlookers, though no one had attempted to help the dog under the deck. I got down on my 70+ year-old hands and knees and saw he was about 20 feet away from me, as far under the deck as he could get. I asked if anyone could crawl back in there and offered to direct them on what to do, but nobody wanted to help.

With no alternative, I fetched a blanket and some cheese from my car and asked if someone could at least pull me out on the blanket once I leashed the dog (my hands would be too full to crawl out). But again nobody would help. Desperate, I asked, "Could one of you *gentleman* please go get the lady who called me?" Apparently that was easy enough.

At least the woman who had called was helpful. She and another lady prepared themselves to pull me out on the blanket, as I went spelunking under the deck. The ceiling was low and the space claustrophobic. When I came close enough to throw the dog some cheese, I noticed he was emaciated and dirty, and he was dragging something on his left front leg. As I crawled closer and offered more cheese, I saw what was bothering him—his leg was caught in a trap!

The dog appeared to be in severe pain, but I could almost bet he was not going to hurt me because his tail would wag from time to time. I put a whole piece of cheese in my mouth and said in a mumbled voice, "Okay boy, I am not going to hurt you if I can help it." I got right up in his face, and he took the cheese out of my mouth. At that point I knew I was going to get him out of there.

I asked the ladies to pull slowly on each corner of the blanket. I needed to hold the leash in one hand and the trap up off the ground in the other so it wouldn't cause the dog additional pain, so the women had heavy, dead weight to pull. The bystanders still just stood around, gaping, as the women hauled us out from under the deck. And when it came time to ask for help lifting the dog into my car, I wasn't surprised to again find myself alone.

Well, this Boxer boy needed a vet, and I was going to get him to one, with or without help! I really do not know where the strength came from, but I counted to three, said a quick prayer, and up into the car went the dog (trap and all).

It was almost quitting time when I arrived at the vet, so no specialists were available to see the dog. None of the remaining people were strong enough to remove the trap, so they gave him pain meds and sent us off to another veterinary office that could help us immediately.

I went inside to get help removing the dog from my car at the next vet and, in the few seconds I was gone, the dog managed to eat most of the cheese and almost half of the bread loaf! This guy was definitely hungry. After removing the trap and giving him a careful examination, the vet decided to keep the Boxer for a few days. He updated the dog on vaccines, gave him antibiotics, fed him, and tried to restore some blood flow to his damaged leg. It didn't look too promising, but good nutrition and antibiotics would give the dog a better chance of getting through surgery.

While the Boxer was recuperating at the vet's office, I had some time to look into the dog license he was wearing when I found him. As his story unraveled, his past became more and more distressing. It turns out the dog had been found by police in an empty house with a torn bag of dog food after the neighbors called them about a dog crying. He was taken to the pound, where he was then released back to his owners after they simply updated their dog license (no questions asked.) So after obtaining the family's new address from the pound, I zipped over to their house unannounced.

The family met me at the door and appeared very sad when I told them I had their dog. They lied directly to my face, saying that their Boxer had gotten away from them when they were at the library. I suggested we go to the vet to discuss their dog's injuries, stuck them in my car so they couldn't flake out, and we were on our way.

The family's reaction upon hearing the costs of caring for their injured dog was typical. They immediately began complaining that they couldn't afford to pay that kind of money "for a dog." Having experienced similar situations many times I knew just what to do…

I took the family (both adults and their two children) to McDonald's. They thought we were only having lunch, but I was actually about to give them just what they wanted—a way to get out of caring for the family pet they never should have had. As we finished our lunch, I said, "Would you like me to take Boxer boy and pay for his care since you're unable to?"

"Oh yes, we would," they answered (big surprise), and I just happened to have an owner release form with me, ready for them to sign. With our business together through, I returned the family back to their home and have not heard from them since.

The Boxer had surgery to remove his left front leg (including the shoulder). To this day he remains one of the most wonderful Boxers I have ever known and is everybody's friend (both human and animal). Oh, and he's not just anybody's Boxer boy anymore... He's my *Clayton.*

 *Mary Nevius*

A "Snort" Break

So What if His Breath Stinks? One of our first fosters, Iain, had holes in his feet, heartworm, intermittent liver and kidney functions, loose teeth, and scars all over his body. Oh, and he was emaciated with *awful* breath! We didn't know what to expect: Would he be okay with our kids? Food aggressive? Friendly? This mess of a dog turned out to be the easiest foster ever... But he never found another home. We kept him! Iain's breath still stinks, but he's gained much weight, and his spirit is spectacular. He sleeps with his head on my son's pillow each night and spends the rest of his time seeking attention on the couch by pawing at us gently. He is the only dog in our home that doesn't require a leash, and he's had no formal training. Seriously, what more could we ask for? -*Whitney Ricciardi*

Don't Believe the Hype: When Patrick went in to pick up Betty Lou, he was told she really didn't like men and had an attitude to boot. From the end of a catch pole (aluminum rod used to catch dogs from a safe distance), she looked up at Pat with soulful, brown eyes as if to say, "Please get me out of here." Pat quickly removed the catch pole, attached a leash, and knelt down to greet this sad and tired Boxer. Betty buried her head in his lap for some much needed ear rubbing, gave him a gentle kiss, and they left the building! Humph. -*Lee Mitchell*

Moments to Remember

It was a hot summer Sunday when I broke the news to my family: I had an emergency and would be late to our yearly Father's Day get-together. Not fully understanding my reasoning, my family carried on without me, and they were shocked when I showed up over an hour late with my newest foster, a very skinny and timid young male Boxer.

Reese was the product of a backyard breeding business and had received little socialization during the entire 11 months of his life. It was apparent he had been doing nothing more than living in small caged area that must have been secluded from humans and other dogs. Sadly, the poor guy's only human contact was probably when the breeders had fed him, so Reese became my challenge over the next few months.

For the first three weeks my mission was to earn Reese's trust. I kept him separated from the other fosters at my house in order to provide a smooth transition from living outdoors to living inside with a family. He was also separated because he had picked up a horrible upper respiratory infection from the shelter where he was held before I got him.

While nursing Reese back to good health and helping him pack on pounds with good food and nutritional supplements, I spent time with him at the door of his crate, begging him to trust me and showing him that I was different from the other humans he had encountered. After three long weeks, I was overjoyed when Reese stuck his paw onto my hand outside his crate. At that moment I realized there was hope for me in earning the trust of this handsome Boxer boy.

One by one, I began to introduce Reese to my crew, and each day I noticed small improvements in his health and behavior. Before long we were going to the park, swimming in the creek, and meeting new people whenever we had the chance. Though Reese was still shy, he was beginning to see that most humans are kind. He even began to play with the other dogs here in his foster home.

About three months after taking in Reese, I did a home inspection for the Criders. From a conversation with our adoption coordinator, I knew they were interested in my sweet Reese, but I didn't tell them I was his foster mom. I just prayed and prayed they would choose Reese because I truly believed they were the perfect forever family for him.

My prayers appeared to be answered because the next day that wonderful family called our rescue, requesting a time for their dog and Reese to meet. I was so happy; I was in tears at the thought of my Reese finding such a great home. Our meeting was a success, and though Reese didn't want much to do with them at the time, the Criders understood he would warm up to them in due time.

It wasn't long before Reese, now Sawyer, went to live with his new family. The Criders promised to not only love Sawyer, but to be understanding and patient with him as they earned his trust, just as I had done. Before they drove off, Sawyer looked at me from the car as if to say, "Come on in, there's room for you here, too!"

I gave him kisses and whispered, "Now Reese, we've had this talk, darling. It's time for you to go to your forever home so I can help another Boxer in need. Be a good boy, I love you!"

As the perfect family drove away with their newly adopted Boxer boy, they told me not to worry; they would send pictures and keep me updated on his progress. Again I found myself shedding tears of joy. These perfect moments, when everything falls into place, always make the challenge of fostering worthwhile.

 *Shannon Walker*

One Woman's Trash...
Another's Treasure

Sam was surrendered to his veterinarian in the prime of his life at six-and-a-half years old. Ironically, that same vet had been trying to convince Sam's owner to surrender him to Boxer rescue for about a year.

Sam's owner had told the vet that she really didn't love him and had never bonded with him, but it wasn't until Sam presented a head tilt, unsteady gait, and stroke-like symptoms (including half of his face sagging) that she decided to get rid of him. She didn't even care enough to authorize the vet to do any diagnostic work to figure out what was wrong with Sam; she just dropped him off and walked away. I later learned she went to our local puppy mill within a week and purchased a new Boxer puppy.

After the vet's office contacted our rescue, my first thought was that Sam probably had a brain tumor and would not be long for this world. But upon meeting this happy-go-lucky guy, I knew he deserved a chance. At least he deserved someone to love him unconditionally for whatever time he had left. We said we would take him and asked the vet to get to work figuring out what was wrong. It turned out not to be so simple, as Sam had no tumors, and his blood work was fine. All we could do was to start him on a large dose of antibiotics and small dose of prednisone (steroids) and cross our fingers. Three weeks later we weaned him off the prednisone, and miraculously Sam became the picture of health, never again experiencing similar issues.

My family and I were just fostering Sam. Our male Boxer had passed away about a year earlier, and we weren't really looking for another Boxer just yet. But fate has a way of giving us just what we need...

For us, what we needed was Sam. This dog, who had never been loved and cherished before, found a home that accepted him for what he was: a funny, loving, easygoing guy who didn't ask for much. He was happy with just a full food bowl, a good ear rubbing (at least every night), and a soft couch to sleep on. Sam was a true testament to the Boxer breed and the senior in need. He helped remind my family and me about unconditional love, living each moment to its fullest, and acceptance. When we adopted Sam, we knew our time with him would be limited, but Sam lived for four more wonderful years—years my family will treasure.

 *Lee Mitchell*

Lessons from the Unadoptable

I have a roomy kennel with ample space for unsocialized dogs to ease their way into society, so Blue Ridge Boxer Rescue asked me to foster and evaluate a Boxer named Ripley, who appeared to be blind and very unsure of humans. This four-year-old dog had been saved from a shelter and was in boarding until the rescue could find him some space, so of course I said I'd be happy to help.

On the way home from visiting my in-laws in Virginia, my husband and I stopped in Hickory, North Carolina, to pick up our new foster. Ripley turned out to be a funny-looking Boxer: short and skinny with small, cropped ears. In all honesty, he was pretty pitiful.

When I leaned over him to say hello, he snapped at my hand. It was not the warmest greeting I had ever received. As I sized him up and remembered that we had taken my husband's pickup and not my usual SUV with dog crate, I thought, "Okay, this is going to be a challenge."

Getting Ripley into the cab of the truck to sit between us was tricky, and the three-hour ride home to Charleston, South Carolina, was very tense. Poor Ripley had no idea who these strangers were, where he was going, or what was in his future. He was clearly uncomfortable, but who could blame him?

The first week was touch and go, but only one other time did he snap at me. I had been pushing him from behind to get him into his kennel, and he wasn't keen on the idea. Luckily I managed to get my hand out of the way in time, but I had to make a mental note to watch myself around him.

As I said, Ripley was mostly blind. He had *progressive retinal atrophy*, a hereditary disorder causing afflicted dogs to eventually lose all sight. Rip could only see small shadows out one eye when I first got him, so he had to use all his other senses to get around.

Even though blindness, neglect, and abuse had made this world a scary place for Ripley, at some point he figured he had to trust someone, and that someone turned out to be me. I worked hard for his friendship, sitting outside his kennel and talking to him for hours, telling him how handsome he was and what a good boy for not snapping. I fed him twice a day, and he finally started responding to my voice after several weeks. I knew he was beginning to trust when I saw him start wagging his nub at me when I came by.

Ripley was making progress and never showed aggression to other dogs, but even after several months he would still snarl and bark at everyone except for me. This is a harsh reality that fosters and rescue volunteers are sometimes faced with: Ripley had to be deemed "unadoptable." Our rescue couldn't risk him injuring a human, so Ripley would have to be put down.

Sometimes, however, rescue volunteers are able to make a different choice, as was the case for me. I knew I had the space, and after several months Ripley had come to trust me to care for him and love him unconditionally, so I couldn't let him be euthanized. Since dogs are pack animals and generally crave human companionship, living in a kennel is usually less than ideal. But for Ripley, I figured it was a better choice than death, and on top of it, our kennel is no ordinary kennel. It has six indoor/outdoor 8 ft. X 20 ft. runs and two large paddocks where the dogs can exercise.

I was glad to save his life, but thinking of Ripley never having a home of his own, never experiencing the warmth of crawling into a bed with sleepy humans, broke my heart. I decided to try and assimilate him into our home with our other four dogs by kenneling them next to him during the day when I went to work. They all seemed to get along, and after several months I felt comfortable enough to bring Ripley into my home. My wonderful husband, Kevin, was hesitant because Ripley was still aggressive towards humans, but he didn't have the heart to say no. Instead he just gave Ripley his space and didn't try to force a friendship, which was the best thing he could have done. You see, Ripley couldn't see with his eyes, but he could see into a person's heart, so it didn't take long for him to become best friends with my husband. (I suspect all the yummy treats helped a lot!)

Though Ripley eventually went blind completely, you would never know it. Once he knew his area, he never ran into walls. Since we lived in the country with lots of open land, I would take him and his kennel buddy, Rosie, for walks off leash, so they could run. What a sight to see him running at full speed and thoroughly enjoying himself. He was fearless of what was ahead and quickly learned to trust that when I said, "Easy," it meant he should slow down or change direction. What a smart guy! Ripley even learned to navigate around the pond, taking an occasional dip when he needed to cool off.

For three years Ripley did get to experience the warmth of a human bed, sleeping between my husband and me. Though we had very little company during that time and had to medicate Ripley for skin and thyroid conditions, they were very fulfilling years. Ripley was a great guard dog, and I think he truly appreciated our efforts to give him a loving home.

Life with Ripley was going along smoothly until one day we noticed a lump on his leg, and our worst nightmare came true: Ripley had *mast cell cancer*. Several months and three surgeries later, our hearts were breaking. Ripley also had a large, inoperable tumor in his abdomen, and we could no longer watch him suffer. Kevin and I held Ripley in our arms and told him what a good boy he was as he passed on to Rainbow Bridge. He was with us for such a short while but will never be forgotten.

The valuable lessons we learned from Ripley will stick with us for a lifetime and are worth sharing. First, put your heart into it when you're running, and go full speed. Don't worry about things you can't see. Yes, you might run into a few obstacles, but you can back up and go around them.

Second, it's what's in a person's heart that truly matters most.

Third, everyone needs at least one special friend to depend upon. No one can go it alone.

Fourth, even a small dog can steal a piece of your heart if you're not watching.

The week after Ripley passed I was reading in my bed with *all* the other dogs sleeping around me. The night was silent until I clearly heard the tip-tap of doggie nails on the hardwood floor coming down the hallway towards my bedroom door. My female, Merlot, also heard it and went running off the bed and out of the room. I could see her in the hallway, between my room and the kitchen, where she stopped dead still and sniffed the air, wagging her little nub. I am convinced what we heard was Ripley coming back to say goodbye...or maybe he is still with us.

 *Kay Peters*

A Friend in Need

Bonheifer is a talkative (I love the talkers), gentle, loving, senior but his days are numbered because of a nasty brain tumor. A wonderful family, the Stricklands, adopted him last year, even after the vet told them in November he would only have a few months to live. Well, it's now the New Year, and he's still hanging in there. Bon is not in any pain, but his head tilts completely, and he has lost quite a bit of mobility.

One day some friends visited the Stricklands with their dog, and Bon was so happy. He got up and played (as best as he could), so the Stricklands decided to adopt another dog. They knew this would make Bon's last days as happy as could be.

I was assigned to the Stricklands as their adoption counselor since I had helped them the first time around. Bon's dad, Don, reminded me of their preference for brindle males, but I told him I only had a brindle female at the time. He said they were open to meeting any dog—they were just looking for someone to invigorate Bon. I was concerned that the dog in question, Kendra, was shy and timid, but when I mentioned it to Don, he simply replied, "Sometimes so am I."

Kendra shined during their introduction, and she seemed like a perfect fit. Bon perked up and went outside with her, where they followed each other around the backyard. The Stricklands said they had not seen that much wiggle from Bon in a while. Bon was such a happy boy with Kendra around; it was one of the best adoption experiences I have ever had.

I saw the Stricklands again today, and they told me Kendra and Bon had an instant love for each other. When Don opens the backdoor for Kendra, she goes back to the living room to get Bon. Bon then gets up and she patiently waits for him to go outside. She is amazing with him and his limitations. The Stricklands said they went on three walks today, and Bon was just so happy. He even went upstairs, which he has not done in some time. He has the sweetest little tail nubbin wiggle. They are so sweet—all of them.

Today was a good day for me—one I will never forget.

 *April Robbins*

Deaf but Not Disabled

My story begins one year ago last October. It was a cold, wet day and I was all alone wandering the streets. I didn't know where I was going or how to get food, and even if someone called to me to offer something, I couldn't hear them because I am deaf. It seemed I was destined to walk the streets scared and alone. That is, until I looked up and saw a man with a stick coming towards me and thought things might be getting even worse. After putting a rope around my neck, he placed me in a truck, and we rode for some time before reaching our destination, which for me was a wire kennel.

Not knowing what would happen next, I shook with fear. It appeared I was in a place where someone could find me and take me to their home, but who would want a deaf, filthy dog? Some people gave me food and water, and it wasn't cold like the streets were, but I still felt a foreboding danger.

After a time the answer to my question still seemed to be, "Nobody." I was eighteen hours from my world coming to an end when a lady finally came into my kennel. She leaned over and touched me, and I could feel her love and caring in my heart. Was I actually getting a chance for a better life?

The woman took me home that day into a life I had only dreamed of. I was timid because I thought the love I was receiving from this woman was too good to be true. But God does answer prayers, for shortly thereafter I went to my forever home, where I now receive even more unconditional love (even when I make mistakes).

My forever family doesn't even care that I'm deaf. Mom has shown me that she can talk to me by making signals with her hands. She calls it "sign language." I know fourteen signs and it has opened up a new world for me. Oh, and guess what? My new mom takes me to schools and foster homes for children. She tells people my story, and we show them how we communicate with each other. I must do a really good job because I'm always rewarded with cheese.

As if life weren't good enough, we are about to embark on another adventure! I soon will begin therapy dog training, so we can go into hospitals and make sick children happy, just like we do for the kids in foster care. I want to get my story out to the world, for you see, I am deaf but not disabled. My mom says being deaf just makes me *very* special, so maybe when others meet me, they'll want to give other special dogs a chance, too. (Hint! Hint!) Mom and I assure you, dogs like me can and do make a difference, and we won't let you down!

River, translated by Trish Locklair

A "Snort" Break

I'm Real: The female with cropped ears was the opposite of what I was looking for but turned out to be more than I could have dreamed of! Hana's nicknames say it best: "The Wal-Mart Greeter" (because she welcomed everyone she passed), "Hana Banana," "Marble Eyes" (because her eyes were so big), and "J-Lo" (because a she had such a big booty that was always wiggling)! Hana always allowed me to dress her up for rescue events. From the fairy to the clown to the maid, this girl was always so tolerant. I personally think she enjoyed dressing up, but others might beg to differ. - *Michelle Trotter*

Not All Divas Are Dames: Sleek and slender, "socks" painted to perfection, Bodie (Bodacious the Bull) went on a spa vacation with Teresa and me. One look at our room and Bodie voiced our silent disapproval with non-stop whining and pacing. After calling my boy Bodie a "Diva," Teresa phoned up the front desk and explained that the room was not what she had seen in their advertisement. The people were very accommodating and moved us to a luxury cabin overlooking the lake! No whining and pacing here; it was a room fit for a Boxer. - *Ty Merrick*

Pay It Forward: At 12 weeks old, Sidney found herself in a shelter with a horribly broken leg and an angel looking over her. She was taken into rescue and this angel, a veterinarian, fixed Sidney's leg and also nursed her through pneumonia at no charge to us, only asking that we "pay it forward." Did we? I'd say so. After careful screening, the perfect forever family is now living happily ever after with their beautiful, brindle girl, and we've gone on to save many, many more. - *Gail Traylor*

A Superficial Love Affair

Remington came into my life like a shot. I was studying feverishly for an advanced math final, the last final of my college career. During breaks I checked my email, hoping our rescue group had found a Boxer for me to adopt.

On this particular day, I received an email from a friend with this short message: "I think you need to see this boy." I looked at the picture she had included of a beautiful Boxer boy named Brutus who was the spitting image of Booker, our rescue president's reverse-brindle male whom I was in love with. His owners had dumped him, so his time at the shelter was limited, and he was at risk for euthanization. Even though I tried my hardest, I couldn't study during the rest of the night, and I had trouble sleeping. Brutus was stuck my mind.

The next morning my boyfriend (now husband) and I were at the shelter when it opened. I had a small window of time before I needed to be back up at the college for my final. When the doors were unlocked, we bolted in and immediately saw the beautiful Boxer we had come for. Brutus went outside to relieve himself and got very muddy running around the small side yard. It was clear he was most interested in getting away from the shelter.

In the meet-and-green room, Brutus was a *maniac*! He couldn't sit or stay, and he wanted to French kiss us (which meant jumping up and smearing mud on us on us to reach our mouths). My boyfriend gave me a look, and I knew he was second-guessing my excitement. Deep down I knew Brutus' behavior wouldn't guarantee me an angel, but I was blown away by his beauty. Pair this shallow love and his crazy behavior with the fact that he would be my first dog ever, and most would have called this adoption "doomed."

Nevertheless, we brought Brutus up to the front of the shelter and announced that we wanted to adopt him. It was a very swift signature and exchange of money, and we were on our way. My boyfriend loaded Brutus into the truck, and we raced back to my college, so I could take my final. During the exam I couldn't wait to get home to see my new boy.

I already had a new name for Brutus before we ever met...Remington. My uncle always had Golden Retrievers with gun-themed names, and I thought that was cool, so I followed his lead. But honestly, Remington didn't care what we called him as long as he was out of that shelter.

Remington hasn't changed a whole lot since then. He loves being outside where he does Boxer burns (running feverishly in circles and figure 8's) like nobody's business! He can be found sunning in the backyard on warm days. We joke that he must be solar powered and needing to recharge. He is the almighty protector of our home, cornering the meter reader and several maintenance men and scaring off more people than we know. Of course he would only lick them to death, but his looks are enough to deter any miscreants. He is jumping up on us less, but he forgets his manners around strangers. Remington's beautiful reverse brindle coat has become a little gray in the five and a half years we've had him, but he's still the gorgeous boy that I met so many years ago, inside and out.

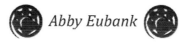 *Abby Eubank*

Z is Just the Beginning

My husband and I had been looking at Boxers for a couple years off and on. My aunt had adopted from a Dachshund rescue and suggested we look for a Boxer rescue in the area. We found the Midwest Boxer Rescues website that services our area of Iowa, so I filled out the online application. I thought for sure we would hear back quickly because there were many dogs available on their website.

To my surprise, I waited and waited but didn't hear back. When I finally called to see how long this was going to take, I found out that the dog run in my yard had pushed my application to the back of the pile! The rescue said we were unable to adopt because homes with runs usually had the intention of keeping dogs in the yard all the time, which was unacceptable. With this new knowledge we immediately offered to take it down (it was there from the previous owners of the house), which would then re-qualify us to adopt.

Once we had it removed, the rescue sent a woman and her Boxer to inspect our house and property, and we passed with flying colors. The conversation quickly turned to questions about the type of dog we were looking for and what we expected, and the next few weeks involved back and forth phone calls. We ultimately picked a dog named Isaiah... in Kansas!

So the time had finally come to go get Isaiah. We started our drive at 4:00am with three little kids and a dog crate in the car. Six hours later we arrived at the foster home, wondering if this was indeed the dog for us. We weren't left wondering for long, as Isaiah greeted us at the door and then jumped on my husband's lap as if to say, "Where were you? I've been waiting so long for you!" And that was it. The foster and I shed a few tears as Isaiah jumped up into the Jeep and away we went.

Many people change their dog's name upon adoption, but we stuck with Isaiah. A nickname has emerged, however, and he's mostly called "Z" for short.

Z is everything we wanted and more. Everyone who comes over wants to take him home because he is so easygoing and game for anything. All he wants is to be with the family and receive attention. He is also known as the "garage dog," not because he lives in the garage, but because when the guys are in the garage, Z is right there with them. He has his own truck seat to sit on and watch while they work. When it's warm in the summer, he lies in our bushes next to the garage while he watches the men tinker. He also lies on the floor with the kids, watching cartoons. The only trouble with Z is that we occasionally have to remind him that a 60-pound dog does not belong on our laps.

When we adopted him, the foster said at first they thought Z would have to be put down because of training issues. We are so glad they didn't give up on him because not having him in our lives is unimaginable. Z is such a wonderful gift, making everyone feel good, especially on our bad days, because he is always waiting excitedly at the door every time we come home.

Z was just the beginning of our adventures with rescued dogs. We have since adopted another Boxer, a female this time, and her and Z are the best of friends. They often get into trouble together, but that's part of the fun, right?

 *Jennifer Anderson*

Will Hug for Love

There he was—big, brown eyes looking up at me, fawn-colored and handsome, sitting on the cold snow, tied on a short leash to a pole in their driveway, pee and poop surrounding him. The volunteer that did Tyson's evaluation told me that he had not been walked for one year. The owners surrendered him, saying he was unable to walk on a leash, so they tied him to the pole for several hours a day. In the cold, rain, heat, snow, no matter what, that poor boy was outdoors, which was no place for a Boxer. He was wearing a harness that was so tight it took the fur right off from under his neck and left him with welts. I was horrified. I went inside the house to get the paperwork signed and to take this boy to freedom. I would be his foster mom.

I sensed Tyson knew I was there to set him free because he looked at me with those sad eyes and wiggled his butt; he couldn't wait to get into my car. We headed directly to the pet store for a bath (he was so dirty and smelly), and he kissed me the whole ride.

I later learned that the home from which I had retrieved Tyson was his second, and he'd been neglected at the first one as well. In that home he was left in a crate from Friday through Sunday with one bowl of food, one bowl of water, and nowhere to relieve himself but in his bed. This poor boy had been through two terrible homes, but he still had kisses to give me.

After Tyson's bath we went to my house, where I took him into the backyard and let him off his leash. He just ran and ran around the fenced-in yard, and I cried my eyes out—Tyson was finally free. He was grinning from ear to ear as I gave him a toy, and we joyfully played fetch. Given his history, where he learned the game I don't know, but he played like a pro. It was if he had never had this freedom before, but he had been thinking about it for a long time.

I was instantly in love with this boy, and there was no way I could give him up. So on our fourth day together, I contacted the Boxer rescue and requested to adopt him. They said yes, and it was one of the best days of my life. Tyson had found his forever home.

Now Tyson has been with me for three years. After learning some basic manners and social skills including walking on a leash, he passed the AKC Canine Good Citizen test. He then became a certified therapy dog with Therapy Dogs of Massachusetts. We regularly visit Alzheimer's patients, assisted living facilities, and kids with emotional problems, and everyone who meets Tyson loves him.

Tyson shows his gratefulness to me every day with kisses and hugs. Yes, hugs! He actually gives hugs by pushing his head into your body, and you can't help but hug him back. I knew I could give Tyson a wonderful life with walks, play time, treats, and lots of love, but I never thought that rescuing a dog would give me such a wonderful feeling. It's really the best thing I've ever done, and I will always be thankful for my boy Tyson.

 *Lisa Barker*

Devotion, Love, and Loyalty

W e went to the pet supply store to buy food for our dog at home, *not* to get a puppy. But a rescue group had several crates lined up outside, and we couldn't ignore the skinny, small Boxer curled into a ball at the far corner of her crate. Her precious eyes looked up, the tail she was not supposed to have started wagging, and I was a goner right then and there. My husband, well, he took a little longer to warm up to the idea. As we debated and discussed, my two small children fell in love, so it was a battle my husband lost before it really even started. Nine days before Christmas, Ella the unexpected Boxer came home.

Ella is a beautiful fawn, with a white chest and smudge on her nose. She was eleven months old when we met her, and her life had been spent tied to a trampoline by a frayed, filthy rope around her neck. She was starved, neglected, and beaten. To see any animal in such a state is simply mind-blowing. Ella still has scars—the ones we can see, and the ones we cannot.

Seeing our scared little girl wag that whip of a tail as if nothing were wrong is remarkable. Her spirit, her ability to love us and trust us, is the truest testament to the gift a dog gives us humans. Ella (a.k.a. Ella-Boo) is a blessing that someone tried to destroy. We can only shake our heads and ask why. As my friend always says, "Who raises these people to do such things?"

Ella has proven herself countless times as a sweetheart, a precocious puppy (we have *plenty* of proof of that), and a loyal, true companion. I have always believed dogs know more than we give them credit for. Ella showed me just how much one Sunday night in April.

That morning, our beloved Australian Shepherd, Sparkle, had passed away. She had been with me since college, when I started to lose my eyesight and decided I would rather have a dog keep me safe than a cane. Sparkle and I were a team, but that did not mean Sparkle loved only me. She put up with my college years, our two kids pretending she was their horse, a stray cat she adopted and cleaned, and of course, Ella. When we came home with Ella, Sparkle gave me a look that said, "You must be joking." I was worried there would be some adjustment problems, but unless you count Ella immediately labeling Sparkle as "Mom" and Sparkle immediately labeling

Ella as "Kid," we had no problems at all. Ella followed Sparkle's lead, which was amazing to watch, really. With as much training as Sparkle had received, Ella could not have had a better example from which to learn. For two and a half years, I watched the two girls and their bond. It was strong and obvious to anyone. They protected each other, played with each other, and yes, bickered with each other.

When Sparkle got sick with kidney failure, everything changed quickly. Ella knew something was wrong and became gentler with Sparkle. She lay beside her and napped instead of playing. Somehow our sweet Boxer girl knew Sparkle was dying.

The day finally came when we no longer had any choice in the matter. Sparkle was done. She told me she could live no longer, and we made the hardest, most painful decision in our lives. As we left the house, Ella sat stoically at the base of the stairs, her eyes watchful, her tail still, and her ears up. She knew.

That night I sat on the floor in my bedroom, holding the harness and collar of my best friend of eleven years. Ella quietly came and sat beside me. She carefully sniffed the collar, cocked her head to the side, and gave me her soulful, sweet stare. I burst into tears. Heartbroken and devastated, all I could do was cry. Ella placed her velvet soft head in my neck, blew out a warm breath, and stayed that way. How long I cried, how long we sat there, I do not know. I wrapped my arms around her, buried my face in her soft fur, and wished I still had both of my babies.

When I finally lifted my head, Ella looked at me with big, wet eyes and tears on her smashed-in, little face. It was obvious she *really* knew. She knew her friend was gone; she knew Mommy was sad. *She knew.* That chilly April night Ella sat and grieved with me, connecting with me in a way that cannot be described with words. Her heart hurt, too, it was right there for me to see. She needed comfort as much as I did. The connection we had only grew stronger, and we helped each other in a way that can only be understood by the two of us.

Since Sparkle left us, we have adopted another Boxer, but I have not sought another guide dog. Sparkle was special, and I have to say that even with time it has not been easy.

Devotion cannot be measured, neither can love nor loyalty, but you can *feel* them, as I did with Sparkle, and do with Ella, every single day. When we go for walks, Ella has unofficially taken on some of Sparkle's guiding duties, watching over me, walking a sure line in front of me, making sure my path is safe.

I hope everyone has a chance to feel and see the wonderful gifts dogs give us. Every time I look at Ella, I see them. Every time she comes to me, I feel them. What a blessing she truly is. I have to ask myself who saved who sometimes.

 *Anonymous*

Birthday Surprise

After losing my Boxer to *cardiomyopathy* (a deadly heart condition), I said I wouldn't get another because they just take pieces of you with them when they pass. Then, three years later, my husband was approached by a co-worker who asked if he wanted a Boxer puppy. She said they couldn't handle their 12-week-old, out-of-control puppy and were going to take her to the pound. My husband, knowing I would be in heaven, picked up the puppy that afternoon and brought her home to me as a birthday *SURPRISE!*

We promptly named her Dixie Belle and she was everything her previous owner described. She was completely out of control, and not house or crate trained. She ran through the house like a freight train and left destruction in her wake. She terrorized our other animals. My husband called her our "crack baby."

We thought that as the years went along she would mature and calm down. NOT! Dixie was a pistol. She thought that all toys—especially balls—were meant to be destroyed, and she'd tear them up within minutes of having a new one. Dixie loved basketballs and would bite them for weeks until they popped. (Unfortunately her basketball fancy also wore teeth down to nubs.) Tether balls, which Dixie would jump and hit for hours at a time, were a joy for her, too. The game only ended when I'd bring Dixie inside to prevent her from having a heart attack from playing so hard.

Dixie had a zest for life. She loved playing in the water and had her own baby pool. She ran in the rain and loved playing in the mud. Snow was also a great favorite as she thought it was a gift from above and ran around trying to catch each flake.

The way we acquired Dixie raised our awareness about the many Boxers languishing in shelters, which eventually led us to start Rockin' "P" Boxer Rescue. We have since taken in and found homes for about 1,000 Boxers.

Dixie went to the Rainbow Bridge in December, two weeks before her eleventh birthday. Her legacy lives on through Rockin' "P," even though she is missed greatly.

 *Angie Persch*

A "Snort" Break

What About Bob: I absolutely fell in love with Bob, my second foster, a big boy I often refer to as my "Big Tub O' Love." After bonding through heartworm treatments and aggression issues, I had not realized how much I wanted to keep him until my husband gave me a birthday surprise. The card he handed me said, "I guess every dog has his day." Insignificant in and of itself, until I read what he had written below it: "...and today is Bob's." I did not understand at first, but my husband had seen it before I had—Bob belonged with us. *-Anonymous*

Pushing Our Buttons: Chancy likes to push our car's buttons. He rolls down the windows and makes the DVD player drop down from the car ceiling (though he's always disappointed when we're not showing *Lassie*). It's all very amusing until he locks you out of the car on Christmas day and your keys are still in the ignition... Chancy's button-pushing does have it benefits, though, like when he turns the flashers on for us in a crowded parking lot. I guess he doesn't want to take a "chance" on losing this family!*–Teresa Reid*

A Matter of Perspective

Craigslist Ad: *Free to anyone with more patience than I have. Two-year-old Boxer puppy. Does not come when called, but her name is Abby. Missing back left leg, so she can't scratch her left ear. We ask her every day where her leg is, but she won't tell us. In spite of her handicap, jumps on furniture and runs in a circle like nothing I've ever seen. Loves toys - anything loud that squeaks. Bugs the crap out of you by dropping her ball at your feet, then grabs it and runs off when you bend down to get it. Shoves toys under the furniture, then whines until you fetch them for her. Abby loves to pee all*

over the rugs in the living room and dining room; however, she saves her poops for the kids' bedroom carpet. Will eat anything she can get ahold of. However, only weighs 40 pounds because she is bulimic. Is not picky about where she throws up. Loves to fight with our other dog and, despite the fact he outweighs her by 100 pounds, can kick the crap out of him. Does not sleep and will wake you up to play at 4:00 a.m. if not in her crate. Fights to the death when you attempt to put her in her crate, so oven mitts or thick gloves and a sofa-cushion shield are required. Yes . . . her bite is much worse than her bark. Has been spayed and is up-to-date on all vaccinations.

First, I wonder whether this ad is for real. My curiosity turns to anger when I realize the ad is referring to our sweet tripod rescue, Abby. I can't be mistaken because the accompanying picture is one we had posted in our adoption ad on Petfinder.com when we were in the processing of find Abby her *forever* home.

I immediately call the woman who had adopted Abby and very kindly remind her of the adoption contract she had signed, which states if an adoption does not work out for any reason, the dog is to be returned to our rescue. She agrees to relinquish Abby back to us, so my friend, April, and I immediately go on our way.

Only having the Craigslist information to go by, I'm expecting a crazy dog tied up in the back of an SUV. Instead, I find a cute little "baby" Boxer seat-belted next to her giant Boxer brother. "Wait," I think, "doesn't she try and kill him?"

As soon as Abby is out of the car, she comes bounding towards us with kisses for April and me. I look at the woman's hands, expecting them to be mauled, but there's nary a scratch. Abby hops in my lap, exerting some dominance, and with a quick correction she's back to Boxer kisses. Instead of goodbye, the woman wishes Abby "good riddance," calling her "rotten" in a tone that flips my stomach.

Now the time has come to test Abby's boundaries. April picks her up and puts her in the kennel single-handedly (her other hand is bad)—not one growl, not one raised hair, not one bit of a fight. Abby did fine in the crate and had no problems in the car.

At home I arrive to chaos as my boyfriend (at the time), Anthony, has let out all my dogs: the obnoxious puppy, the submissive pup, the Napoleon-complexed little dog, the hyper male, and Hugo, who runs the house. It looks like this is the perfect opportunity to find out if Abby is truly aggressive, so with fingers crossed I watch as Abby meets each dog and backs down in every confrontation without a second thought. Not one scuffle.

I can't help but laugh as I write about her because Abby is lying next to my bed giving Hugo the eye. Not the evil eye, the "I'm completely infatuated with you" eye. She loves attention and cries for it, but I make her earn it all (there are NO free lunches in my home!). One "no" to the crying and she is lying on Hugo's dog bed next to mine. It's obvious that some love, discipline, and exercise are all this dog needs.

A few weeks pass and nothing changes—Abby is still loving and friendly to my dogs and me. None of the horrifying behaviors so vividly depicted in the Craigslist ad have emerged.

It turns out Abby is quite the social butterfly and very creative in her attention-seeking. She proved it to me one weekend when we were doing yard work. I ran inside for a lemonade break while Anthony raked out new mulch in the yard. When I returned, Anthony was grinning ear to ear with Abby cradled in his arms like a baby....and his shorts around his ankles! It turns out Abby had been pestering him, so he had played with her and then continued working. I guess when he turned his back she saw her opportunity to hook her paws in his waistband and pull herself right into his arms, pushing his shorts down as she climbed up. What a sight for sore eyes!

The lesson from this story is that you can't believe everything you read. Had Abby written the Craigslist ad, it would have said something like:

Funny, loving Boxer princess, running away from impatient, intolerant bitch (pun intended!). Looking for attention and more attention. Will help with yard work in exchange for love.

The second time around, a wonderful family answered Abby's adoption ad (not exactly the one above). They love her to pieces and don't even care where her leg went. No oven mitts or sofa cushions required...

 *Whitney Price*

Abuse, Rescue, and Malice

 alice is now six years old, but I remember the day I got him like it was yesterday. I had just moved into an apartment with my Husky, Atreyu, and I wanted to adopt a Bully breed-mix puppy. Atreyu and I went to Petsmart that day, and in addition to the treats and goodies we were looking for, we found a rescue group adopting out the most beautiful Boxer I had ever seen. I fell instantly in love with her but thought I should get a male because Atreyu was a female.

A rescue volunteer knew of a Pit Bull "rescue" that had Boxer/Pit Bull puppies for adoption. It sounded like just what I wanted, so I took down the rescue's information and called as I left the store.

That evening I went to meet the puppies. It was pitch black outside, and the directions given to me by the woman with whom I spoke led me down a long, dirt road. I was so excited to meet the puppies that the similarities of my situation to certain horror movies escaped me.

All I had for navigation was a white mailbox; there were no streetlights and no signs. After missing the mailbox once, I started thinking that I had found the bad part of my new neighborhood. Upon turning into the "rescue's" driveway, my stomach instantly knotted into a ball, and the truth became apparent. In front of me sat a rusty, old trailer with no skirt and countless broken-down cars. Trash was strewn around like yard art, and the echo of dogs barking bellowed through the property like a zoo. This looked more like a puppy mill than a rescue.

I stopped the car dead and seriously considered turning around. I didn't, though, because an invisible paw seemed to be pulling me forward. I hesitantly made my way up the wooden steps to the door, knocked, and was blown away by the smell of urine when the woman opened it. Apparently oblivious to the nauseating, eye-burning scent, the woman and several frenzied dogs greeted me and hurried me to the kennel room.

Looking around I couldn't believe the sight. Crate upon crate, containing dogs and puppies along with days' worth of urine and feces, were stacked everywhere, and in the filthy kitchen I could see a mommy dog with her litter of tiny puppies. My eyes welled with tears, and my head filled with all sorts of things I wanted to say to this "rescuer," but I kept my emotions locked inside.

I approached the six tiny, ribby, orange and white Boxer-mix puppies I had traveled to hell to meet. They were all piling over each other, slipping and sliding in their urine and feces, in a crate that was way too small. I picked up the tiniest of all the puppies, who had the sweetest little white nose with black speckles. He immediately kissed me, and I knew I was taking him home. I figured if I could save one puppy from this "rescue" it was going to be him.

The "rescuer" apparently had not neutered, microchipped, or vaccinated the dogs, yet she required a $100.00 adoption fee. And although this establishment, this "rescue," was clearly nothing more than a scam, I paid the fee, filled out the paperwork, and ran out the door with my new puppy as fast as I could.

At home my heart sank when I bathed my puppy and the bath water turned red from all the fleas and feces coming off him. I dried him off and we cuddled in bed, falling asleep until morning. The next morning I was given a new surprise: My puppy's bowel movements were full of blood. We raced to the vet where the puppy was diagnosed with a severe hook, round, and whip worm infection, coccidia (intestinal parasites), and severe dehydration. He was hospitalized for two days.

After seeing where he was born, I guess I shouldn't have been surprised. I wrestled with my disgust, wondering how that woman could possible call herself a rescue, and I vowed to my little "Malice" boy we would somehow make a difference for dogs like him.

Since helping Malice get healthy, he has never left my side. He graduated from puppy, basic, and advanced obedience classes and has never required a leash. He's closer to me than any best friend I've ever had—a true ambassador for the human/canine bond. To think he just might not have made it if I hadn't taken him home that night is devastating, and I can't bear to wonder what happened to his brothers and sisters.

Unfortunately I know for a fact that the neglectful woman who sold me Malice is still selling dogs, under the guise of a "breeder" instead of a "rescue" these days. Despite my best efforts I haven't yet been able to shut her down, but I won't stop fighting. Because no dog should have to go through an experience like Malice's, I'm now saving dogs, one by one, through Rugaz Rescue. It's a *real* rescue, where dogs are vaccinated, altered, microchipped, and then sent on their way when the perfect match is found...and not a second before. In the meantime they are loved and nurtured in clean, happy homes where the only things lining the walls are furniture.

 *Devlynn Saunders*

Beirut Benji

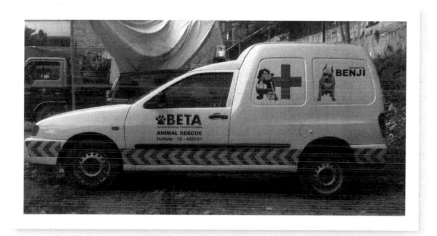

As the unofficial Boxer sanctuary in Beirut, Lebanon, we often receive phone calls about animals in need. On this particular day it was our local rescue group, Beirut for the Ethical Treatment of Animals (BETA), calling to ask if we could take another Boxer. Obviously the answer was yes, but where to put him was the challenge. We already had Harold, who was given to the rescue because he has deformed feet, and Muttley, who was found running down the main highway to Beirut. Both dogs were seven, and while wonderful in their own rights, these two boys fought when put together.

We took a deep breath, surveyed our property, and picked a safe area for Benji. He arrived soon thereafter, and moved into his compound in the garden with the stable block as his gentleman's quarters. But what a sight he was! He had a large bandage wrapped around his abdomen like a cummerbund, as he'd recently had a huge tumour removed—something like the size of a six-inch eggplant. Benji had been found in a car park, starving and wasting away, and he looked so lost. Plus he had a broken toe.

Two-year-old Benji made a very good recovery, and, in due course, he plumped out to be a normal shape and size. He was never without his trademark massive, plastic bone, which my parents brought out to him from Cumbria, England. These bones are about two feet in length, and Benji loved to play with them in the garden.

In winter Benji would spend more time in the house—well, the kitchen to be more precise. One of my daily duties in our house is that of chef. At about 7:30pm, I go to the kitchen to start my prep for the evening's meal. Because of his presence in the kitchen on cold evenings, Benji became known as my sous chef. Our maid, Lucy, always said that Benji had a watch. At 7:30pm on the dot, if I wasn't already on duty in the kitchen, there would be a big "OOF" followed by more "OOFS" as Benji became annoyed by my lateness. Once I was present, he would sit back, relax, and enjoy his chew bone. Every night!

Sadly, he fell ill and died from a growth on his liver. We only had him for two years, but he was very special. More importantly, they were two years of pure pleasure for him.

Distraught and wanting to memorialize Benji in some way, we decided to donate a van to BETA. It's adorned with Benji on both sides and states, "Donated by Benji."

Since we lost Benji, we have added two girls who love the boys to the pack. There's adorable, four-year-old (we think) Bessie, who had been starved and thrown out of her house, and Blossom, who at almost a year was just about to be put down. As the need continues, "The Sanctuary" will remain open to Beirut's Boxers for many years to come.

 *Michael Dunn*

Blown Away

I was fairly new to fostering when I was asked to take a Boxer who had been shot. Of course I said I would, when and if he recovered. The first pictures I saw of the boy, whom I would name Magnum, were horrific. I couldn't believe he was still alive, and my amazement was shared by the doctors.

In the next few weeks he had two surgeries, and I went to see him several times while he recovered. Magnum was sweet, but something was missing. He didn't have that Boxer spunk I had come to love. There was no spark in his eyes and no Boxer wiggle. If I wanted to pet him, he would let me, but I had to go to him. Occasionally he would share a small kiss with me, but it wasn't the Boxer kisses to which I had become accustomed.

Regardless, I was overjoyed when I got the call that Magnum was ready to come home. Magnum, however, didn't seem to share my enthusiasm. He didn't perk up at all as we walked to the car, and even when we arrived home, he seemed withdrawn and disinterested.

Over the next several weeks, as Magnum's wounds continued to heal, I came to know him better. It didn't take me long to figure out that he had spent very little time, if any, in a house. My suspicions were confirmed one day when he got behind an open door and couldn't figure out that if he simply went around it, he could go outside. He was also far from housebroken. In fact, at times I felt that he was completely backwards. He seemed to consider *outside* his house and *inside* his potty!

It was also obvious that Magnum had had very little human contact. When called, he rarely responded, and he seemed completely unaffected when people would pay him attention or pet him. While my other Boxers craved attention, Magnum couldn't care one way or the other. At night when our family was watching TV and the other fosters were competing for their places next to someone, Magnum was in another room sleeping in a chair by himself. Magnum didn't even show interest in greeting visitors at the door.

As the months passed and Magnum's physical wounds healed, his emotional wounds began to heal, too. The more attention we paid him, the more he seemed to enjoy it, and he started to come out of his shell. He even began to get that Boxer wiggle when someone came to the house. His natural (uncropped) tail moved like it had never moved before.

I wasn't at all surprised when we went to a pet fair and a couple fell in love with my sweet Magnum. They seemed perfect and passed our application process with flying colors. Although a part of me dreaded the thought of Magnum leaving, I was very happy he had found his forever family. The plan was for the family to pick him up after returning from a two week vacation, but when the phone call came, the news was not what I had expected. For reasons beyond their control, the couple said they were not going to be able to take Magnum. As I told them how sorry I was, I felt a smile crossing my face. Something inside me was jumping up and down, and when my boyfriend got home from work, I couldn't hide my joy in telling him about Magnum's adoption falling through.

When I get a new foster, I always remind myself that he or she will only be here for a while, and I am just a step on their way to their forever home. But that night as I looked at Magnum, as he snuggled next to me on the couch, I knew that Magnum's forever home was right here with me.

When I look at Magnum now, it's hard to remember the wounded Boxer who first walked through my door. My Magnum has his Boxer spirit back. The spark in his eyes now can light up a room. When we come home at the end of the day, Magnum is the first to meet us at the door, with his tail wagging as fast as it can go and his whole body wiggling. When I sit on the couch at night to watch TV, Magnum is always right next to me, covering me with kisses before snuggling next to me to go to sleep. Gone is the aloof Boxer whom I met at the veterinary hospital. In his place is a sweet Boxer boy who loves everyone.

When someone asks me how I can foster Boxers, it doesn't take me long to answer. There is no greater joy, at least none that I can imagine, than knowing I have helped give a living creature a second chance at life. When I see that spark return to their eyes, as I did with Magnum, I want to see it again and again. Rehabilitating them and then letting them go (usually) is worth the gift of unconditional love that is the spirit of a Boxer!

 *Lorie Tomlinson*

That Jazzy Feeling

I was in a rush! I desperately needed a dog. Or more correctly, Peanut did, before he died of heartache. I had just put down Esha, my 13-year-old, German/Australian Shepherd mix, and then a week later we moved to a new home. Peanut, my miniature Dachshund, was lonely *and* disoriented. He always looked so sad when I got home from work, and when I put a voice-activated recorder in the house to see what he was up to when I was gone, I found out that he cried for about four hours out of a nine-hour day.

Why was I looking at Boxer rescue in particular? I'm not really sure, but now I'm glad I did. I went to a few Boxer adoption days at local pet stores. The dogs were all beautiful, but I never got that *feeling*. Then I found out about a rescued Boxer meet-and-greet that was to take place an hour from my house the following weekend, so I packed my high hopes into the car and went for a drive. Again, all of the Boxers were beautiful, but I still didn't have *that feeling* about any of them.

Upon leaving, I thanked the organizer and mentioned my struggle in finding the right dog. She suggested I hang around for a few more minutes to meet a brindle Boxer who was still in the van. They had just picked her up from a shelter only hours before she was to be put down. I was hesitant, but I followed the woman to the van, and when she opened the backdoor I felt it! Jazz was standing there, wiggling her little nub and biting at the cage, desperate to come out and meet me. I knew right then that the dog standing before was meant to be mine.

I begged the lady to let me take her home that day, but Jazz still hadn't been spayed and brought up to date on her shots. The woman said Jazz wouldn't be available for two weeks, which was a problem because Peanut was so lonely, but I had no doubt that Jazz was the girl for me.

A week later the rescue brought Jazz to a meet and greet closer to my home and asked me to bring Peanut to make sure they would get along. Peanut likes bigger girls, so I thought they would be fine together....and they would have been, had some careless child not thrown a chewie between them (a big no-no when introducing dogs).

Despite their small tiff, I was still confident we could make it work, so Jazz came to live with us a week later. I was right, and without any chewies to compete over, it didn't take long for Peanut and Jazz to become the best of friends.

Peanut has since crossed the Rainbow Bridge, and we have adopted a sweet, funny, white Boxer named Buzz. As for Jazz, I'm still really not sure why someone gave her up. Her coat is beautiful, and she's been a great dog: well-mannered (crosses her legs like a lil' lady) and unconditionally loving towards my family. Whatever the reason, I'm glad they did because I have enjoyed the last seven years with her. Jazz the Boxer, just like jazz like the music, has a special way of making everything feel happy and right.

 *Debbie Johnson*

A "Snort" Break

A Crate Built for Two: On our first day with Lily, I placed her in her crate, put Riley (our other Boxer) in his, and headed off to work. I know I locked both *metal* crates when I left, but Lily still met me at the front door when I returned home. From the warmth of the carpet near Riley's cage, I determined she had chewed her way out of her crate so she could be closer to Riley! From then on, the two lovebirds were crated together in a Great Dane-sized kennel. I knew they were happy because Lily never tried to escape again. *-Monique Tagliavia*

Not So White Anymore: Winter Lily, my white Boxer who was said to be deaf but is not, is an avid fetcher and will play until we make her stop. She just can't get enough of that tennis ball. She enjoys playing in the rain, which creates mud, providing the perfect situation for a doggie mud bath! We've also got to watch it when we let Winter Lily out to potty in the rain; she's been known to return with a mud mask! She gets it perfectly set on her face, with hints of white peering through around her beautiful amber eyes. *- Amanda Hislop*

Sometimes Everybody Wins

A breeder was looking for someone to euthanize Benjamin, a four-week old pup, and she thought I might be the gal for the job. She was so wrong. Naturally we had no intention of putting him down, and instead we took him home.

Seeing him that cold February day over a decade ago is etched in my mind. He was a frail, smelly, and disfigured dog with green mucus oozing from his mouth and nose. Upon further examination, my husband discovered he had a cleft palate with a rather large opening. It was a weekend, but this poor dog was desperate for medical attention; the infection and drainage had to be cleaned out. After being involved with rescue for so many years I have become quite resourceful, so I got out my dental water jet (never to be used again) and cleaned most of the infection drainage away. I then sank a stomach tube into him and gave him a nourishing solution of half water and half goats milk to help him gain some strength.

On Monday the vet advised me to keep doing just what I was doing, and we started Benjamin on antibiotics, too. About a week later we added puréed dog food to the goats' milk. As Benjamin quickly grew bigger and stronger, I knew I had to make some decisions about him being adopted out, but my heart nearly stopped every time I thought I would have to part with him. He was such a good dog.

One day I took another rescue to a vet at Ohio State University for heart testing. While I was there I asked if they knew anyone who did maxillofacial surgery on dogs. While Benjamin had vastly improved from when I first met him, he still had a hole in the roof of his mouth and facial distortions from the cleft palate that needed repair. The vet looked at me oddly and said, "Are you sure you want to do that on a rescue?"

She wasn't trying to be hurtful, but I couldn't hold back the tears. Seeing my distress, she asked me to wait a minute and then left the room, returning shortly thereafter with a woman who would be graduating in June and returning to New York to start her own practice. She examined Benjamin and said she thought she could help him. Because of her imminent departure and the fact that Benjamin would need several surgeries to correct his deformities, she asked, "Can you leave him today?" I couldn't believe our luck!

I left him, and the wonderful vets at OSU worked their miracles. My heart sang with joy that we were actually able to help Benjamin—and so quickly! As he healed, his true handsomeness was finally revealed. The surgeries were effective and Benjamin just looked great.

During Benjamin's recuperation a rescued Boxer named Maggie mothered him and became his best friend. She was adopted by a gentleman named Doug Thompson, who loved her and felt uncomfortable leaving her home all day while he worked. Would I babysit? Sure! From then on Benjamin looked forward to every weekday because his girlfriend Maggie would join us while her dad was at work.

One Friday evening Doug asked if he could take Benjamin home for the weekend. I didn't like that idea at all because he was my Ben, and I loved him with all my heart. At the same time, I knew it would be good for both Benjamin and Maggie to interact together in a different setting, and they were in good hands with Doug. I let Benjamin go, and as you may have suspected, Benjamin's visits to Doug's house slowly became longer and more frequent. Ben finally made his forever home with Doug and Maggie.

To this day Ben still joins me on weekdays with his new friends, Sadie and Clayton (Maggie has since passed). In essence I've had a wonderful boy for nearly 14 years, but have also had the joy of seeing him adopted into a loving family. As a rescuer I've always had an ebb and flow of dogs through the house, so Doug adopting Benjamin was a wonderful gift. It's truly given me the best of both worlds.

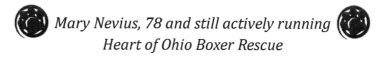

*Mary Nevius, 78 and still actively running
Heart of Ohio Boxer Rescue*

Success Story

Those big, fawn eyes, a puppy mill girl that spent her life in a cement cell. We had to pick her up and carry her to the car, can you imagine? She had never been on a leash, never been on a walk, never been outside, never had a chance to run.

We got her home, sweet and so afraid, not wanting us, not wanting love, for she never experienced kindness from human hands. When I put a hand out, she cowered, and our hearts broke. She loved her furry siblings but had no idea how to play or run with them.

We had her spayed, there was a blizzard. Poor Eva hemorrhaged. Eva was going to die. They operated again, stopped the bleeding and gave her four blood transfusions. She was a fighter and stabilized. They said to take her home for she was too stressed there, and as a miracle, she was so happy she walked on leash for the very first time. She made it, what a spirit. And she now has accepted us loving on her. She came through all this as a dog, a Boxer with a wiggle butt.

This is what this rescue does, it gives everything so these dogs have a chance to be what they were born to be—loved. If we can give them that chance, even if only for a short time, we are successful.

 *Linda Potts*

Forrest Stump

We lost two Boxers within four days of each other. One we returned to the rescue from which we had adopted him after much soul-searching, crying, and hand-wringing, because he was unpredictably, *seriously* aggressive toward our senior male Boxer. We'd never surrendered a dog before and were heartbroken. Tragically our old boy dropped dead of an apparent heart attack only four days later, so we were left with our little, feisty, dynamite-in-a-small-package female Boxer, Wren, who was in a terrible funk and clearly missed her companion.

I searched on Petfinder.com and saw the most precious, mis-marked Boxer face *ever*. His name was Boone, and he was approximately five years old. He was labeled as "special needs," which I immediately thought meant something terrible like heartworm or a heart condition. But upon reading his bio, I found that his only issue was that he had three legs instead of four. Was that all? Whew! I thought his needs were going to be *special!* I contacted the rescue group, Castaway Animal Rescue Effort (C.A.R.E.), to find out more about Boone. Another of my rescue friends remembered having seen this boy at a local animal control facility in October, so why was he still available for adoption in late December? Was he a difficult placement, or had he been adopted and returned?

C.A.R.E. told me that Boone had landed at Springfield Animal Control in October after being pulled from someone's pond. Boxers aren't always proficient swimmers, so I can only imagine how this poor, three-legged boy had struggled. He was already neutered (clearly at a fairly young age), and his left rear leg had been amputated long ago. He'd obviously been a valued pet at some point, as his people had invested a lot of money in his various surgeries. *Surely someone would come looking for this special boy, wouldn't they?* Nobody ever did, but C.A.R.E. accepted him into their rescue program, so he could actually have a chance at finding a family.

C.A.R.E. nursed Boone for two months through a serious upper respiratory infection and skin infections until he was healthy enough to become available for adoption. So the reason he hadn't been adopted sooner wasn't because he was a bad dog; it was purely medical, and Boone was now finally healthy. The news kept getting better and better.

We made arrangements to meet Boone and took our little Wren with us. We were so excited, as we'd not only fallen in love with his face, but he was reportedly one of the sweetest Boxers C.A.R.E. had ever seen. When we walked into their adoption center, all the dogs were barking, bouncing, and demanding attention. It was as chaotic and loud as you'd expect in any type of shelter. We found our "Boone boy" sitting properly at the front of his gate, staring up at us, not making a peep. It was as if he were saying, "You're here, and I'm ready." We took him out for introductions to Miss Wren, and he was very patient with her—to the point of actually ignoring her. It was a perfect match!

For the first week Boone was here at our home, I truly thought he was deaf. Our Boxers have always been very vocal, but the deaf dogs I'd been around always seemed quiet—at least when noises would generally stir or arouse a hearing dog. This boy never made one sound and almost seemed dazed by his surroundings. Maybe he just couldn't believe he had it so good? As Boone grew accustomed to our routine and to Wren's antics, he finally found his voice.

We have since found Boone to be the sweetest soul, a gentle goober of a boy, and he's a dog who never meets a stranger. His goofy, all-white face, with what appears to be a brown aviator's hat covering his head, only adds to his charm. Always vying for affection, when we stop petting Boone, he slowly, gently reaches up his paw to plead for more. He gently bumps you with his muzzle for attention, with a rapid, repetitive tapping motion that reminds us of a bobber jiggling when a fish takes its bait. Or it could be canine Morse code for "pet me!" Boone also loves his crate, a warm fire, and any available cushy bed. Fortunately, he has several to choose here!

This boy truly appreciates all of life's simple pleasures. Because he is such a happy-go-lucky, dorky, "life is like a box of chocolates" boy, we changed his name to "Forrest." We sometimes jokingly refer to him as Forrest Stump, but he doesn't mind. Contrary to his adoption ad, he doesn't have *special needs*—he is just *special*...period. When you watch Forrest run (and can't help but narrate, "RUN, Forrest, RUN!"), it's hard to believe he only has three legs. He is lightning fast and fearless to boot. We've had visitors who didn't realize Forrest was missing a leg until they met him a second time.

The series of events that led us to find Forrest were devastating. To go from three dogs to one in a matter of four days was practically inconceivable. But had things not transpired that way, we'd never have been looking for Forrest. I often wonder how Forrest ended up in that pond and why no one came to reclaim him, but I also feel like these events were part of his destiny. Finding Forrest was our fate, and we will treasure every day we have with him. Just like Forrest Gump and Jenny, we go together like peas and carrots.

 *Karen Rodgers*

Blessed by a Princess

My heart lodged in my throat when she came into view. Inside the exercise pen, nestled on the emerald green grass, lay the saddest, most depressed-looking dog I had ever seen. Her head was down, eyes fixed with that thousand-yard stare into nothingness. She was completely withdrawn from the world. Her fawn coat stretched across her hips and ribs, and scars littered her black face. She looked battle-worn and world-weary. I couldn't even breathe for fear of sobbing.

She had been rescued from a puppy mill (a large, commercial, breeding farm where parent dogs suffer in chicken-wire crates while their puppies are sold in pet shops) that had recently been disbanded by the state. Over 100 dogs and puppies were dispersed to shelters and rescues across Kansas. This ten-year-old girl had obviously spent most, if not all, of her life in that dismal existence, and her time at the shelter had run out. The vet who spayed her found that her uterus had at one point ruptured, and then it had healed on its own. It was a miracle she was still alive.

I wasn't looking to get another dog—I had just buried Stella, the canine love of my life, after a sudden attack of bloat took her from me—but this girl needed me, and I think I needed her, too. I named her Jahzara because it means "blessed princess," and I was determined to treat her as such.

Jahzy was only with me two and a half years, but in that time she knew nothing but soft beds, steady meals, and gentle hands. As time passed and her body healed, her personality began to shine through. She made each dog we fostered feel at home and, despite her petite fragility, she ruled the roost. Not one of them challenged her position of authority. I let her do pretty much anything she wanted; I figured she had earned the right. This included waking me up each morning by pecking me in the eye with her chin like some over-sized hen. Her ears perked up, and I saw joy in her eyes as she demanded my attention. I've never been a morning person, but she always made me laugh before I could even crawl out of bed.

It was a privilege to witness Jahzy's playful nature, such as when company came. As soon as the doorbell rang she would go hide in my room as if afraid someone would take her from me. Then she'd sporadically appear to make laps through the house, greeting each person politely, before running back to my room and waiting for them to go.

One October day, just minutes after I arrived home from work, Jahzy was running joyous laps around the living room when she collapsed and died almost instantly. I held her and cried over her, my face buried in her neck until the last bit of warmth had left her body. The vet later said it was a heart attack. She was almost 13 years old. In the beginning we didn't think she would even last a month, but she seemed to grow younger with each passing day and showed no signs of slowing down.

I often said that while Stella had only lived six years, each day was filled with love and security. As much as it killed me to lose her, if Stella had lived, Jahzy would have died, never knowing what it was like to be loved. I'm thankful to have been given the chance to love them both.

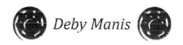 *Deby Manis*

A "Snort" Break

Plowed Out of Bed: When we adopted our daughter Shaneece's foster dog, Dozer (think bulldozer!), we were unsure of whether we could fall in love with such a big, rambunctious dog. But this one's got big eyes, a goofy smile, and a personality to match. Who would have thought we would cherish every moment of hanging off the edges of our queen-sized bed while our snoring dog rumbles like heavy machinery in the middle—but we do! -*Shana Pieprzyca*

A Jolly Good Time: AJ's first Christmas was spent at the vet's office while he recovered from a broken leg and dislocated hip. His second Christmas was much more exciting—he spent it discovering how much fun it is to un-decorate the tree and chew up wrapped gifts when no one is looking. We're sure he was just looking for the giant rawhide Santa left for him in his very own stocking. Next year we'll make it easier for him to find that first! -*Melissa Young*

Easter Egg Hunt: I don't wait for Easter to get my dogs out on the hunt. I keep my plastic Easter eggs on hand year round so I can fill them with smelly treats and hide them around the house or yard. I make sure the dogs know the scent but do not see where I hide them (that would be too easy). The only thing that tops this game is a visit in the yard by an Easter bunny! –*Angie Persch*

Angels Come in Many Shapes

One Saturday I received a phone call about a Boxer named Heidi from a far-away woman who had obtained my phone number from someone who knew I was involved in rescue. In a tired voice she explained she was too sick to care for eight-year-old Heidi and was hoping I could help her. I took down the woman's information and agreed to meet with her the following afternoon.

When a friend and I arrived at the woman's home on the other side of our state, she greeted us at her door. She was bald, wearing a bathrobe over pajamas, and exhausted.

Cancer was consuming her, and she did not want to see her beloved dog, whom she had raised since she was a puppy, euthanized in a shelter. Because of Heidi's age, she knew her chances of adoption were slim.

Heidi was at the woman's side, looking at her with big brown eyes and seemingly listening to every word. The woman and I discussed how our rescue works. I told her that we meticulously screen applicants and take care to place dogs in the right homes so they do not get bumped around from home to home.

After explaining everything, the woman completed the surrender forms, and I took Heidi in as a foster. She bonded with me very quickly, and after a month, she refused to leave my side when we went outside. In the house she always positioned herself so she could see me. I adopted Heidi when she refused to go down the walkway with a friend of mine and instead waited for me on the front step.

Heidi has now been with me for three years. She mumbles instead of talks and does the "mashed potato" whenever I return home. She still won't leave my side when we are outside on our property and shows her gratitude in her own way every day. I wrote her owner a letter when I adopted her to tell her Heidi would be well cared for. I hope it brought her peace to know that her faithful friend had found a loving home. I could not have a more loyal dog; Heidi is an angel in the shape of a Boxer.

 *Elaine Pacheco*

Love at First Lick

"Are you sure you want to adopt a dog?" my dad asked me seriously. "They're a big commitment."

Dad was right, and adopting a dog was going to be a big change from life with just two cats. Cats are easy— you don't have to worry about being home to let them out or walk them, and they can take care of themselves while you go off on a weekend trip. But I wanted a dog. I grew up with dogs, and so I know that there's just nothing like a wagging tail and lolling tongue greeting me at the end of the day. I had wanted a dog for a long time, but I made myself wait until I left apartment living behind for a house with a yard. Less than a month after I moved into my new house, I put in my application with two Boxer rescue groups, crossed my fingers, and waited.

Every day was agony as I waited for my application to be processed, my home visit to be completed, and finally to hear from foster parents who thought their dog might become my dog. By the time I was approved to adopt, I had every dog on the rescue website memorized and a long list of dogs I wanted to meet. Waaaaaaay at the bottom of that list was "Alton." He met some of my requirements—he was the right age and cat-friendly—but I was set on getting a female, and I preferred the flashy fawns (fawn with white markings on the face, chest, and paws) over Alton's plain fawn coat. Plus, I love "class clown" Boxers who will run, jump, and make me laugh all the time, and Alton just looked so serious.

As one dog after another was crossed off my list for one reason or another, I finally agreed to meet Alton. "After all," I told myself, "I might as well get some practice meeting dogs, so I'll know when I find the right one."

Alton turned up on my doorstep one cold December night with a bright blue scarf wrapped around his neck. His foster parents eagerly told me all about his many talents, but I was just watching him, waiting, still skeptical. He ran around the house sniffing every corner and investigating my cats. He didn't even seem to notice me at all. Finally his investigation ended, and he came back to join us. He bounded right up in front of me and gave me a big smile, followed by an even bigger (and sloppier) kiss. All at once, I *knew*. I hugged him and asked him if he wanted to come live with me and be my dog. He kissed me again, and I considered the bargain sealed right then and there.

Alton became my sweet Casey, and life has never been the same. As Dad predicted, it was a big change. No more going away on last-minute trips or going out after work, unless I figured out what to do with Casey first. My owner's resolve was tested almost immediately, as three days after I adopted Casey we were struck with a legendary Texas ice storm. Schools and businesses all over town were shut down, but I was carefully skating across the ice to take Casey on his morning walk.

Yes, it's been a big change, but it's absolutely been worthwhile. Now I rush home at the end of each day, knowing Casey will be thrilled to see me and go on his evening walk. There's nothing like coming home to a Boxer wiggle. When they're so excited, it's not enough to just wag their little nubbin of a tail—they have to wag their whole bodies! I can't be depressed for long with Casey squirming up in my lap to kiss me, and even a dreary walk in the rain turns cheerful when I have Casey beside me, chasing raindrops and splashing in puddles. Nothing beats snuggling into bed on a cold winter's night with a warm, furry body curled up beside me...even if that furry body is snoring (somehow snoring is fine when it's coming from a dog)!

Life with Casey has been a joy. He may look serious sometimes, but he's got the Boxer personality all the way. I'm so glad I met him, even though I didn't think he was exactly what I was looking for. After all, ours is an age-old story: love at first lick!

 *Andrea Westerfeld*

Wise Old Words

Most won't believe that a Boxer can speak out loud, at least not in a language we can understand. Still, in April a few years back, my frail, old Boxer girl, Rae Rae, spoke as clearly to me as I can speak to you. Her words I did not want to hear, yet in all her years with me, they were the only ones that ever reached my ears and touched my heart to such an extent.

Rae Rae was fighting a long battle with *Cushing's disease* (a pituitary or adrenal disease identified by weight gain, hair loss, and abnormal urination), and her frail body was riddled with old age. Rae Rae was nearly 14 years old, and it was a day-to-day heartache for me to see her in such decline. On that day, in such an unassuming way, she said to me, "There is one in need at the shelter and you should go."

I heard the words, they touched my heart, and I knew. . . I knew. That spring day as the sun shone brightly, I asked her, no, begged her to stay with me. To the very depths of my bones, I knew it was wrong to ask her to suffer for me, but I could not let her go, even if another needed me; I needed her.

Finally Rae Rae's little old body wore out. She had stayed as long as she could to prepare me for her passing. Though months had come and gone, her words were still crystal clear, and despite the aching in my heart, I went to the shelter. I was not ready to open myself up to loss again, as there would never be another Rae Rae. Indeed it turned out to be my Mugsy man.

Mugsy is a white Boxer boy who had been starved nearly to death. His leg had been broken, so he could not stand when he was picked up as a stray. He had spent four long months waiting on me. While I could not give up on Rae Rae, Mugsy had not given up hope that I would remember the words she had spoken so clearly: "There is one at the shelter who needs you and you should go."

It has been a long journey for Mugsy, and the abuse he suffered will always leave some lasting quirks about him. There's no need to worry for Mugsy because my home is no longer just mine. Other Boxers who have needed refuge have found sanctuary here, and now it's Mugsy's turn. Some have come for a short stay on their way to a new forever home; some have needed my tears to help them leave the bonds of this earth. But no words ever spoken have changed my life as that bright sunshiny day when Rae Rae said, "There is one in need at the shelter and you should go."

 *Kathy Becton*

"Kimba, remember..."

I am an animal control officer and an animal advocate, and Boxers hold a special place in my heart. In the spring of 1997, I was reluctantly (because everyone knew I loved Boxers) dispatched out to a house to pick up a Boxer who had bitten its owner; the owner wanted the dog put to sleep.

When I arrived, the man was very agitated and had put the dog in the backyard for me to catch. The man had been bitten badly. The dog was a small Boxer, a deep red female, with a very poor ear and tail crop. She was frantically running around and around in the yard. I started as I usually do—advancing very slowly and positively toward her, but she just aimlessly circled. Finally the man opened the door and gave me a piece of bologna. This caught her attention, and as she hesitantly came up to get it, I was able to leash her. As soon as we left the yard, her demeanor changed, and she became very friendly, jumping up and down as Boxers do. She jumped right into the front seat of the truck and snuggled with me all the way back to the shelter.

Like most dogs, she was very nervous and scared at the shelter. My supervisor came out to see her and reminded me I must not get attached because she was a known biter, and no biters are adoptable. Being held the ten days for quarantine, she did come around somewhat to me, but not to everyone. My supervisor forbade me to take her home, even though she did not act like most biting dogs. But my persistence paid off, and finally he gave in and let me try her at home.

In my care she was nervous but loving. I tried crating her so I could leave the house the day after she arrived, but instead of going in, she turned and bit me quite badly up and down my right arm and hand. I realized I was at least partially to blame, since I had hurriedly pushed her into the crate, and perhaps she had bad experiences with crating. I was so angry at myself for pushing her—I knew better—and she was obviously angry, too.

So we had a little talk. I told her that was her one bite; that was all she was getting. I reminded her I had four other dogs, and she was the low pup on the totem pole. I said I understood that one bite was out of fear, and from now on she couldn't bite or fight again.

She looked at me honestly as if to say, "Okay, I understand and respect that, and thank you for giving me that chance."

Then she kissed me. That was 13 years ago, and she has been one of the most appreciative and loving dogs I have ever had.

To this day when she gets over anxious, all I have to say is "Kimba, remember..." and she stops.

 *Stella Koch*

Thank Heaven for Fairy Godmothers

S ome time ago, in the part of Heaven where Boxers are created, a little soul was wandering around, trying to get in the proper line for having "Boxer puppy parts" assembled. She couldn't see very well and was smaller than most of the other Boxer puppy souls, so it's not surprising that she went to the wrong line. She was scolded and told, "That one...that line over there. Can't you see? That is the line you should be in!"

So the little soul, one day to become Luna, obligingly scampered to "that line over there" and waited...and waited... and waited. By the time it was her turn, it was the Friday of a three-day weekend. The assemblers were tired and had plans to get outta Heaven for the weekend and go camping. They thought they had finished and were closing down the shop until "Little Soul #8265" peeked over the workbench with a happy smile—FINALLY it was *her* turn!

"What?!" grumbled the foreman of the Boxer puppy assemblers. "Looks like we have one more to finish before we can leave."

So everyone scrambled to the parts boxes and grabbed whatever was left. They weren't the best parts, but they were purebred Boxer parts nonetheless. The assemblers had used up almost all the fawn paint and all the white paint, so Little Soul #8265 got lucky with mostly shiny black paint, a few milk chocolate drizzles of fawn, and just a little white for her toes and chest. She was so shiny and pretty, and they called her a "reverse brindle."

Next she went on to the inspection line, where they also wanted to go home and didn't carefully check all of her parts. This didn't matter to Little Soul #8265; she didn't notice that her parts didn't fit quite correctly. All she knew was that she was on her way to becoming a full-fledged Boxer puppy.

Next stop for this sweet Boxer puppy soul was the line where they hand out temperament and personality. This time Little Soul #8265 got lucky. A new shift had just begun, and they had a box *heaping* with those items. The workers on this line were all fairy Godmothers who were happy to stay and work overtime and get holiday pay while they inserted feelings into the Boxer puppy souls. Guess who got overflowing amounts of gentleness, sweetness, and house manners? You're right—it was Little Soul #8265. After being passed around for lots of Fairy Godmother hugs and kisses, Luna (as she was about to become) was placed on a conveyor belt and whisked down to earth.

A family who was looking for a Boxer puppy came to inspect the litter Luna was born into. Luna was petite with *huge* eyes and beautiful, shiny, brindle coloring. She looked perfect, and they decided to take her home and call her their family pet.

Luna was a good puppy (one can only imagine) and was easy to housebreak. The family didn't spend much time with Luna and didn't work on training very much because, let's face it, she had such a wonderful temperament; she was "good" most of the time. While they were not paying much attention to her, her front legs started to grow a little differently (remember, she didn't have the correct parts to begin with). Also, one of her hips was not sitting just right and her eyes were a little off. Finally someone noticed she couldn't see like the other dogs in the neighborhood. Her eyes were big and black, but they also looked like they had waxed paper in them. Someone used the word "cataract," but Luna didn't know what that meant and went on her merry way, sometimes bumping into things and ricocheting off in the right direction eventually.

Her family, the one that told everyone she was "the family pet," decided she couldn't stay with them anymore because she wasn't perfect after all. So one dark night they drove to a shelter and dropped her in the night drop box.

Some nice people heard about Luna, rescued her from the shelter, and took her to a vet where she was spayed and given her shots, but not much else. All foster homes were full, so Luna had to spend a *long* time being boarded at the vet (actually it was only several days, but it seemed like *forever* to Luna).

Her reprieve came when the nice rescue people put out a "Christmas alert" to find Luna a warm place for the holidays. There was a rescue home that had a Nana and a Poppi and a big Boxer boy who was six years old. They said their

Christmas shopping was done, the tree was decorated, and they didn't have anything planned for the holidays, and that is how Luna came to be in their home.

Luna's foster family could see that her parts weren't quite right and that she could see only light. They also noticed she was very sick with a bad cold (kennel cough), very skinny, withdrawn, and afraid. They made a nice, soft bed for her in a crate, fed her yummy food three times a day, and gave her medicine for the kennel cough.

Soon Luna started feeling better and noticed the other dog in the home. She could only "sense" he was there and was afraid. She had heard strange, barking, growling dogs around her when she was kenneled at the vet hospital, and it had worried her night and day. That's why she didn't trust the big fawn boy who lived with the nice people. She decided to give him "what for" to let him know she was a tough cookie, and he'd better just *leave her alone!* They had some fights, and though the big fawn boy was a nice guy, he didn't like being growled at and pushed around by a skinny, little girl who bumped into him all the time.

Christmas came and went. Luna rode on errands in the car with the nice people and decided that she loved riding in the car because it was a safe and warm place where she could wait for the nice people to finish their errands while she napped. After the holidays the house had some great children and grown-ups visiting, and Luna was beside herself with joy and love. The nice people mostly kept Luna and the big fawn boy separated because it didn't seem like she was going to want anything to do with him. Oddly enough though, she didn't mind going for walks with him, and they had a good time outdoors.

Luna heard people talking about "New Year's resolutions" and tried to figure out what that was all about. It seems the people around her were going to "try to do better" in the New Year. Luna was so happy to be with this nice family, she decided she would try to "do better" as well. The big fawn boy seemed to be quite important to them; he was kinda cute on the walks and had a lot of nice toys and soft, comfy beds (one even had a heater!), so Luna made up her mind that this was the thing she could be better at. She could get along with the big fawn boy.

She mustered all the gentleness and sweetness bestowed upon her by her fairy Godmothers, and when she got up the next morning, she went to the toy box and picked out the blue octopus. She shook it, flipped it, and walked up next to the big fawn boy to see if he might like to play tug of war. He wasn't too sure—every time he had offered her a toy, she had growled and snapped at him—but he was a very patient boy and decided to give it a try. They played and played and played. They boxed, they body slammed, and they head butted. When they were worn out from playing, they lay on the carpet gnawing on each other's faces and neck (the ultimate sign of doggie-friendship).

The nice Nana and Poppi were *so* happy at this behavior and so *proud* of Luna and her perfect New Year's resolution that they decided to adopt her. After all, Christmas is a time for giving, and there was nothing better Nana and Poppi could give Luna (now lovingly referred to as "Lulu, the Princess of Quite a Lot") than a permanent place in their home.

 *Marlene Gardner*

A "Snort" Break

The Multitasker: Anghus is a comedian: He chews my young children's toes gently, sending them into giggle fits, chases laser pointers, and bops half-deflated balloons up in the air with his nose until we have tears in our eyes. Anghus is a guardian: He tucks us in and watches over our home when my husband is away. Anghus is a supermodel: He's so striking that one man actually got out of his golf cart during his game to ask us where we got him. Anghus is an ambassador: He's a testament to the fact that people can get a wonderful, beautiful family pet from rescue. Yes, Anghus wears many "hats," but the one he never takes off is "loyal friend."
- Ashley Russell

Say Cheese! Katie was not very responsive to external stimuli and had never before smiled. She was confined to a wheelchair and, with multiple physical and developmental challenges, her life had never been easy. I knew Katie from visiting her special education class with my three-legged therapy dog, Jeffrey, who had knack for touching people's lives. One day Katie's teacher helped her put a hand on Jeffrey's head and pet him, and Katie actually smiled! The smile was caught on camera, so in a sense, we were all rewarded with "Cheese!" *-Rose Ann Dean*

Stubborn Saves a Leg

AJ had a rough start in life, but his stubborn personality has turned out to be his saving grace. Many months ago a scared and injured three-month-old puppy arrived at the vet after jumping out of the bed of a moving pickup truck. One of his hind legs was broken and he had dislocated his hip. The owner surrendered AJ to the vet upon hearing his leg would need to be amputated, though I am not sure if it was due to the financial burden or if they just didn't want to deal with a disfigured dog. Either way it was the owner's fault. AJ had been hurt, and now he was left at the mercy of the vet. Determined not to give up on this wonderful baby, the vet contacted Legacy Boxer Rescue for help.

Ironically, the day the vet was scheduled to amputate AJ's leg, he was called away on a family emergency. When he returned, he saw AJ was actually trying to use the leg, so he thought it possibly could be saved. The vet surmised that AJ's leg would never look completely normal and would most likely develop arthritis, but it would heal and be fully functional.

AJ sadly spent his first Christmas alone in the doggy hospital while his leg and hip healed, but shortly thereafter he was released to the Sullivans, a wonderful foster family. By this time AJ's injury had become only a slight limp, which the vet was certain would disappear as the muscles strengthened. The Sullivans did a wonderful job of loving AJ and training him so he could go on to find his forever home. With each day he grew stronger, and eventually his limp went away, just as the vet said. AJ became a typical five-month-old puppy, running and jumping with no trouble at all.

This is where we come into the story. Our family already had a four-year-old female Boxer named Lizzie, and we really felt she needed a companion now that our children were getting older. We knew it had to be another Boxer due to their incredible dispositions and loveable personalities, and since our first Boxer was from a rescue, we were aware of how many great dogs needed homes. After spending many hours scouring the internet, we eventually came across Legacy Boxer Rescue.

Lizzie's enthusiasm can be quite overwhelming, and the first couple of Boxer foster dogs we met didn't take very well to her. Then came AJ, and instantly Lizzie and AJ were like long-lost friends. He was slightly smaller than her, despite Lizzie being a runt, and they played and chased each other for hours.

We were forewarned AJ's foster parents were very picky and had already turned down a couple of other families. Luckily the foster family saw what a perfect fit AJ was for our family, and one week later AJ officially became ours. His foster mother was very attached and cried upon leaving him, but she knew we would love him and care for him.

The scared, gimpy puppy that left the vet's office a year ago has since become a vocal, stubborn, strapping, 75-pound (and still growing) ball of energy, just as a Boxer boy should be. Though he is now almost twice Lizzie's size, she reminds him daily that she is still the boss. She also serves as his surrogate mother, protecting, loving, and curling up on the couch with him, which is the cutest thing. They are completely inseparable.

No matter where we take Lizzie and AJ, people always stop me and remark about their beauty. They are shocked when I mention that both Lizzie and AJ are rescues. It's hard to believe AJ is the same dog who was abandoned and then scheduled for leg amputation. In his case stubbornness was a virtue.

 *Melissa Young*

Timing is Everything

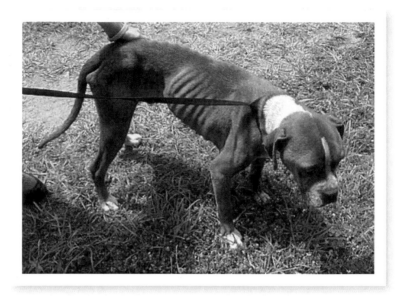

Ben Crafton was one of the skinniest Boxer I'd ever fostered, and he had a laundry list of ailments requiring months of care. He no spark in his eye, and he'd literally given up on life. He just stood there waiting to see what would happen to him next.

Ben was the most recent in a long line of fosters, and they all fit in great with my gang. Not Ben. He didn't care for my dogs, not one bit, so for the next six months I tended to Ben in my spare bedroom. He had his own little palace with a couch, his crate, and toys galore, but that didn't make Ben happy. His separation anxiety caused him to be terribly destructive; he ate my door, the molding, and even the drywall.

But the bond between us grew stronger every day. He started trusting me just a little more, and I started loving him much, much more! After six months I was finally able to introduce Ben to my gang without snarls and snips. We were making progress with socialization, but Ben's health remained a rollercoaster for almost a year. As soon as Ben was over the heartworms, he broke out with lesions all over his body. He was diagnosed with Canine Leproid Ganuloma, also known as canine leprosy. Over the next few months we battled this rare disease as well.

As Ben began to pull through all of his ailments, he became happier and happier and more comfortable at my home. He was finally getting along great with my gang, but meeting new dogs continued to be a challenge. I couldn't even take him to adoption events because of how he reacted to the other dogs.

People often remark that I saved Ben's life, but what they don't know is that he saved mine as well. About two weeks after Ben Crafton came into my life, my husband asked for a divorce. Ben's honest eyes and beautiful soul reached out to me as we would sit together at night and snuggle. My ex-husband stayed out with our "pack," and I stayed in the spare room with Ben, who was my constant companion. Rehabilitating Ben became my "project," and I woke up each day knowing he needed me. Ben helped me remember what my life was all about.

I always thought that I would eventually adopt Ben, but I already had three Boxers and didn't want to add a fourth dog. Ben didn't draw much interest from potential adopters because he's a mixed-breed, very dog-aggressive, and no one wanted a dog with a tail.

Things didn't turn out for Ben how I thought they would, though. A year-and-a-half after he came in to my home as a foster, a potential forever family finally took an interest in Ben. After talking with them on the phone, all I could do was hope and pray they would love him as much as I did.

At their home visit, Ben walked into their house like he had been there many times before. They loved him and felt confident they could handle his behavioral challenges. He now has two kids to play with and a devoted mom and dad.

I am grateful every day that Ben came into my life. The skinny Boxer-mix who started out at 29 pounds grew up to be 58 pounds of pure joy. In retrospect, I don't think it took so long for him to be adopted because nobody wanted him. I think he was just waiting until he had finished his task of helping me through my hard times, and then he could finally move on to his new purpose in life—being a great family pet in his new home.

 *Michelle Trotter*

Just Looking

I have a soft spot for older dogs, the forgotten ones who are always the last to be rescued. Being the sucker I am, when I heard that an eight-year-old Boxer named Cheerio was on death row at the local shelter because she had been there too long, I went to visit her. The shelter worker asked if I wanted to spend some time with her, and I hesitated before nodding; I was just looking, after all.

My husband and I already had two Boxers and didn't need another, so I hadn't planned on even mentioning my visit with Cheerio. But of course, that evening I couldn't resist telling him about the lonely, beautiful Boxer I had met. I was taken by her soft, graying, fawn fur, her deep, brown eyes, her wise aura, and the fact that her life was in danger. He sighed deeply and said what I had hoped to hear: "Go, get her. You know you're going to anyway." I guess he knew me too well.

The next day I went back to the shelter and told the animal control officer I wanted to adopt Cheerio. She was surprised I wanted such an old dog, but in short order the paperwork was finished and Cheerio was on her way to her new life. At home Cheerio became my shadow. She would follow me everywhere and was the best snuggle buddy. Remington and Moe, our male Boxers, would start in our bed and leave before morning, but Cheerio stayed there all night.

Cheerio was adjusting well, but on her second night in our home, she had a seizure. I had never dealt with seizures and didn't know what was happening at first, so I did everything wrong. I tried to move her, I stuck my hand in her mouth, thinking she had swallowed something, and I even thought water might clear up whatever was in her throat.

We rushed her to the vet the next day, who informed us that there was no real cure for seizures. The vet suggested medicine to reduce the frequency, but it wouldn't eliminate the seizures. Instead we decided to just keep an eye on her and go from there. She had a clean bill of health otherwise, and in time her seizures became less frequent. By the time we had had her for two years, they had completely subsided.

Cheerio was as healthy as our other dogs, until one day she acted a little woozy. She had a hard time walking straight, stopped eating and drinking, and frequently fell down. As her figure, or lack of, indicated, she loved food, so for her to be feeling bad enough not to eat was a big deal. The vet gave her two possible diagnoses: a brain tumor or *vestibular disease.* Fortunately she had the latter, which is a doggie version of vertigo. After some shots and hydration, Cheerio's symptoms went away on their own.

The symptoms of vestibular disease would occasionally reappear in Cheerio over the next few months. They would generally disappear on their own, until one night she didn't want to leave the couch and follow us to bed, which was strange. We carried her to bed with us so she wouldn't fall off the couch in the middle of the night, and the next morning we moved her stiff-framed body onto several dog beds we had laid out on the floor. Though Cheerio barely acknowledged us, we had to leave for work.

At lunch I received a frantic call from my husband. Cheerio hadn't moved from where we placed her and had urinated and drooled on herself. I met my husband and Cheerio at the vet and saw that Cheerio's unmoving body was contorted into a strange position. She was still alive, but she was not aware of where or who she was. The vet suggested medication to keep her comfortable, but the episodes she was having would keep coming back with more severity each time. At this point, she wasn't in pain, but it would become painful in the future. We made the heart-wrenching decision to let her go over the Rainbow Bridge.

As we left the office empty-handed, I reminded my husband of the day she came home. She explored our home and yard, tested out our beds, and ate the dog food for her and my two boys. Then she sat down, looked up at me, and gave me one of her rare smiles. She was an atypical Boxer, calm with smaller jowls that weren't big enough to hold any slobber, so we didn't have to clean up after her like we did for our boys. She didn't do kidney beans (the unmistakable Boxer wiggle) and instead stomped her front feet in excitement when we returned home. She didn't do the typical "woo-woo" noise either, and she rarely barked.

Cheerio taught us so much in the short two years she let us care for her. From her example we learned not to worry about what people think about us, not to let age stand in the way of doing what we want, and certainly not to ever turn down love and affection. It wasn't until she was gone that I realized I may have just been looking when I visited the shelter, but Cheerio had already chosen me.

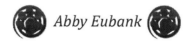 *Abby Eubank*

Sadness and Solitude NOT Allowed

My husband and I loved Boxers. Three bouncing Boxers had graced our home since 1990, and we vowed to always have at least one. Back in September 2003 we were sharing our home with our 13-year-old Boxer, Goliath, and our wild and crazy one-year-old pup, Jack, when our world came crashing to a halt. On September 23rd, 2003, my husband unexpectedly passed away.

Of course the following weeks were just a blur, as I tried to cope with this devastating loss, all the while knowing in my heart that I needed to brace myself for even further heartache. Poor old Goliath would stay just long enough to make sure that Mama and little Jack would be okay, and then he would have to leave us, too.

My fears were realized when, just three short months later, Goliath left us in search of his dad. He had recently celebrated his 14th birthday, and the vet said his big ol' gentle heart just gave out. With our hearts shattered once again, little Jack and I were left alone.

Eventually I had to return to work, leaving Jack alone for the very first time in his life. Needless to say, he did not handle this well, and my heart broke all over again each time the neighbors called to tell me about Jack's pitiful cries and incessant howling as he protested his solitude. I knew I had to do something to help him, but at the same time I sure didn't have the strength or the nerves of steel needed to tackle a new puppy. A dear friend, who volunteered with Boxer Rescue and Adoption, suggested I talk to the rescue president, Dianne, about a companion for Jack. After doing all the application paperwork and getting approved at our home visit, Dianne asked me to bring Jack to her home to meet her rescues. I found that quite surprising and said so to Dianne.

I remember Dianne saying, "Well, of course, the dogs will decide who is right. You didn't think *you* would decide, did you?" I still laugh out loud thinking about this; she was so right. As we let Jack into the room of crated potential sisters, he immediately went to one dog, then to another, then back to the first dog, then to another, back to the first dog, then off to another crate... but he ALWAYS stopped back at the very first crated girl in between visits to the others.

Finally, after watching this for several minutes, Dianne laughed and said that she thought we might have a winner. We took Jack and Girl #1 outside, and sure enough, after a very wild and woolly play session, we had indeed found our "winner." We called her Jaimee, and she literally changed our lives. Laughter had finally returned to our home.

Jaimee is a sassy little girl, full of life, love, and happiness, never hesitating to tell us how she feels or what she wants. She loves to play, play, play, and neither Jack nor I have time to feel sorry for ourselves anymore; Miss Jaimee simply does not allow sadness or solitude. Oh no, there is no place for tears or howling or loneliness in Jaimee's world. She hit the ground running and brought the sunshine back with her. This happy little girl truly returned Jack and me to the land of the living. I guess technically you would say that we "rescued" Jaimee, since after all, she was the rescue dog. But I know in my heart just exactly who rescued who. Thanks Jaims!

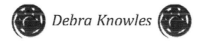 *Debra Knowles*

My Houdini

When my fiancée and I broke up, the only thing I really missed about the relationship was his Boxer, so I turned to Blue Ridge Boxer Rescue for help. Connie, a volunteer with the rescue group, drove about four hours to do my home inspection and introduce me to my potential "baby," Lexi. My previous knowledge of this beautiful, brindle Boxer was only that she was a housebroken, stray dog, who knew a few commands and how to get out of a window (which she had done in a previous foster home).

My home inspection checked out, and Lexi has been with me ever since. But to say it was a rough adjustment at first is an understatement. At 2:30 p.m. on the first day she was home alone, the rescue group and my leasing office called, saying Lexi was found in my parking lot. I was mortified. I lived on the third floor, and when I had left, Lexi was in a crate. It turns out I had failed to lock a little door on top of the crate. (How she fit through that little space, I will never know.) I could tell Lexi had tried to exit the apartment through the windows because all of the blinds were destroyed. She had also tried the bolted front door, as evidenced by teeth marks on the door knob. Lexi had finally managed to open the sliding door and jump over the balcony, using my stored bicycle as a ladder. Note to self: Lock the balcony door.

Lexi escaped with only a small tear to the outer lung lining, which caused her oxygen levels to be slightly lower than normal. The vet said it would heal on its own.

Determined not to let Lexi escape again, the next time I left my house I used zip ties to secure Lexi's crate doors. I shut both bedroom doors and locked the sliding balcony door, fastening it with a security bar. Regardless, at 10:30 a.m. I again received a call from my leasing office that Lexi was in the parking lot. This time though, after drinking some water, Lexi's vomit was reddish-pink. Kristy, the property manager, and Nikki, the assistant manager, agreed to meet me at the vet. Luckily a thorough examination revealed Lexi had only exacerbated her previous injury, and there was no further damage.

Upon returning to my apartment, I discovered that as careful as I had been to zip-tie the doors shut, I had neglected the corners of the wire crate. Lexi had shaken the crate (it was the fold-down kind), until the front had flopped forward. Then in her frenzy to escape, she had managed to knock the security bar down off the sliding door and had gotten the door unlocked.

That night I ordered a Gorilla Tough Crate with expedited shipping from the Dr.'s Foster and Smith website, and the next day we tried doggie daycare. Lexi did well during her first half day, but on her following visit she was expelled for being aggressive with another dog. I was quickly running out of options, but the new crate came just in time. After being zipped up and locked down, I was pleased to report that Lexi was finally safely contained. Or so I thought...

Lexi continued to struggle with separation anxiety, destroying two plastic crate pans and eating chunks of her fleece blankets. I became accustomed to her red, blue, or plaid poops, which was determined by which blanket she had eaten. And then one night it happened again. While I was at the pool, Lexi escaped her crate. (I had only used *one* zip-tie instead of several, and she ate through it.) This time she couldn't use the sliding door because I had reinforced it with four 2x4 boards cut to size, but in her attempt to get out, she managed to lock me out of my apartment. There is no way to access this particular safety lock from outside the apartment, so maintenance had to use a crow bar to get me back in. In the meantime, Lexi had spread trash around the apartment and eaten half of her new bed.

The next day I returned home from work to find what looked like an explosion. Lexi had somehow pulled the partially destroyed bed toward her crate and managed to *thoroughly* destroy it. The cover was pulled into the crate with her, and stuffing was flung about the room. I took a picture of the destruction to the vet's office, and after a good belly laugh, the vet prescribed Prozac to help her with separation anxiety.

Lexi's medication, dog obedience school, and a set routine has made a huge difference. We've been able to wean Lexi off the Prozac, and she still appears to be cured of her destructive tendencies (though she will always be an escape artist given the opportunity).

After that first week with Lexi, the rescue group said they were amazed at my patience and tolerance. In my mind, by signing the dotted line I had committed myself to Lexi for better or for worse. That was three years ago, and while she may still be a little Houdini, one thing Lexi can't escape is the fact that she's stolen my heart. I still believe adopting her was one of the best decisions I've ever made.

 *Lisa Hansen*

It Takes a Village...

Before coming to live with me, Molly spent her days in a Missouri puppy mill's cement block kennel, giving birth to litter after litter of pups who were designated to go to pet stores across the country. Molly was over-bred, under-socialized, painfully shy, and looked just plain scared to death.

After years of "service," Molly's reward was to be dumped on the side of a busy freeway. A passerby alerted authorities after seeing the stray dog, and the hunt was on. It took Missouri animal control two weeks to capture Molly and transfer her to Minnesota Boxer Rescue (MNBR), an organization with a reputation for saving these breeding girls.

When I adopted her, Molly did not know about houses, doorways, or leashes. She kept her head down, eyes averted, and looked like she wanted the ground to swallow her up. We carried her into the house and she immediately sank to the floor. When I tried to gently guide her to another area of the house, Molly crawled on her belly, looking more like a snake than a dog. Her first day with us was spent in the fetal position with her head hidden and an invisible sign on her back stating: "Leave me alone!"

On the way to the vet the next day, Molly panicked and squirmed like a hooked fish out of water. In short order, the collar and leash were in my hand, and Molly was down the street. It was futile to call after her (even though I did) because she did not know her name and was certainly not coming back.

I pursued Molly in my car and enlisted a few policemen in the chase. She was spotted at a local high school a mile from my home and was gaining ground fast. We were just about to give up when a man walking a dog said he had just spotted Molly on the next block. I turned the corner in my car and there she was, running right down the middle of a busy road and headed toward the freeway.

Then she was gone, and there were no more sightings. I had given up on the idea of ever seeing Molly again, but when MNBR immediately organized search groups, contacted hospitals, animal control centers, and shelters, and printed and hung 300 flyers, my hope was restored. Over the next several days we were called with many sightings: Molly scrounging through the trash on the edge of the freeway, a thin boxer drinking from a backyard pond, a dog lurking around some condos. Again and again, team members staked out the area to try to catch Molly.

It looked like we wouldn't catch her, until one day Molly made a gigantic mistake; she took up residency on a very exclusive, private golf course. That got everyone's attention, especially the groundskeeper, Ben. Ben chased her around in his golf cart and found out where she was slipping under the fence to come and go. There was also a large drain pipe Molly may have been using as a hideout. At one point, Ben followed Molly off the golf course and cornered her in a partially fenced area at a local playground. But Molly, the breeder gal who knew no other life than a cement cell, desperately wanted her freedom and again managed to escape.

Day nine finally brought an end to Molly's adventure. She was winded, tired, and emaciated, and Darrick, a wonderful man who loved dogs and had been following Molly's story, was finally able to corner her for the last time. Molly returned to my home, never to run again, but she still had a long road to walk toward becoming a family pet.

As I worked with her, I started to wonder if she might be missing her last batch of pups that were taken away. I thought of the stuffed brindle Boxer I kept on my bed, which had been my companion for all those years I couldn't have a real dog. I decided to give it to Molly, and she immediately started to grunt. Then Molly started to sniff, moving closer to the toy. When I picked up the stuffed dog, Molly stood up. I took the toy to the back door and placed it on the deck. Molly followed.

This went on for several weeks, but how could a stuffed dog teach Molly to eat from a bowl? To walk on a leash? To cuddle up and accept love from humans?

That was when I went back to MNBR and found Stella, a 10-year-old, happy, well-socialized girl, who had a good family life until a divorce forced her out of her home. Stella taught Molly *everything* about being a Boxer.

Today, ten months later, Molly is making progress. She does well walking on a leash, as long as Stella is around. Now Molly is not afraid to go through doorways and play and potty in the backyard, but she is still afraid of shadows and will hide in the corner of a bedroom unless all the lights are on in the house. Molly makes grunting noises but does not bark, instead letting Stella alert us to strangers. Molly still does not play with toys, but she seems to enjoy watching Stella chase a ball around. Molly eats a few bites at a time from her food bowl and then runs and hides, but she does come back for more bites and more hiding. Stella has taught Molly how to jump up on the bed at night and lie next to her humans. Molly will follow Stella up on the couch, and together they watch out the window for me to come home from work.

The greatest joy in my life so far is that Molly allows me to pet her. She will raise her angelic face to mine, and for a moment I can see a light in her hauntingly sad eyes, a ray of hope that life will always be this good. During these special moments, I might also get a tail wag or two, before Molly catches herself trusting a human. She will then run off and hide to compose herself. When Molly first comes back out to visit me again, I will see that hollow, dull look in her eyes. But as my hand stretches forward to scratch her head and ears, the light returns and all is good in the world.

Molly is matronly-looking with her white face, although our best guess is that she is only around seven. She has calluses on all her joints that have worn to leather patches, but she wears them like badges of honor. Her shoulders droop a bit and she slouches when she sits, as if the weight of her past life is almost too much to bear. Her gentle soul shows in every movement she makes. Molly is cared for, comfortable, protected, and wants for nothing.

No matter how far down the road to recovery Molly does or doesn't walk, she will always be loved intensely and infinitely.

 *Lucy Blake*

Boxer Breakfast: Satin Balls

Many Boxers need to gain weight for one reason or another. Feeding your dog "satin balls" is one way of packing on the pounds quickly. This recipe for satin balls is courtesy of Rhonda Carpenter, a foster mom with Legacy Boxer Rescue who had to help her foster, Piper, gain weight before surgery:

Ingredients:

- *10 pounds hamburger meat [the cheapest kind]*
- *1 lg. box of Total cereal*
- *1 lg. box oatmeal*
- *1 jar of wheat germ*
- *1 1/4 cup vegetable oil*
- *1 1/4 cup of unsulfured molasses*
- *10 raw eggs AND shells*
- *10 envelopes of unflavored gelatin*
- *Pinch of salt*
- *Bottle of skin and coat vitamins (optional)*

1) Mix ingredients together.

2) Form into 1 inch meatballs.

3) Freeze in 10 quart freezer bags and thaw as needed.

4) Feed raw. Each meatball is equivalent to about ½ cup of kibble. Recommended to feed 1 satin ball with ½ cup kibble per meal *after* easing your dog onto them little by little (maybe start with half a satin ball first).

Boxer Battles

Piper's leg had to be amputated after she was hit by a car (before landing in foster care). Following her surgery she was pretty depressed, and it probably didn't help that we felt sorry for her. We realized then that we couldn't show that emotion anymore. She  was alive and doing very well, what more could we ask for? We began treating her normally, quit feeling sorry for her, and made her move around and start doing things for herself. That made all the difference in the world. Piper came out of her depression and became the happy-go-lucky girl we had fallen for. After a couple of weeks she was running and jumping and playing with other dogs. To Piper losing a leg is now no big deal at all. *-Rhonda Carpenter*

Little and Lucky: Denney (now Little Man) was the runt of a litter from a backyard breeder. He had a dome-shaped head and wide-set, almond-shaped eyes. At six weeks old he weighed only 2 pounds 11 ounces, and the vet diagnosed him with hydrocephalus—water on the brain. Little Man's chances of surviving were very slim, but we knew he was a fighter. We bottle fed him every two hours, gave him supplements and Omega 3's, and carried him around like an infant *at all* times. That was four months ago, and I am happy to say that, though his body is still producing excess spinal fluid and he requires daily medication, my Little Man is now a happy-go-lucky Boxer, with not a care in the world! *-Judy Eastwood*

Boxer Battles

A Rough Start: When introducing my foster, Bob, to my other Boxer, Jewel, I did it completely wrong. I just brought Bob right into my house and in a second he was on her. For the next 3 months Jewel cowered each time she passed his cage. After getting neutered and having some time to settle in, I decided we should give Bob another chance. After all, keeping two dogs separated all the time is no fun for anyone. I enlisted some help, and had the dogs meet in our front yard after walking separately through the neighborhood. It worked! Even though Bob still doesn't like other dogs, he puts up with Jewel's "boxing." - *Anonymous*

Love is the Best Medicine: Tired, hungry, and in pain, Stella decided to walk in front of a car and see what would happen. The woman behind the wheel, Beth, noticed Stella was bleeding out her behind and took her to a vet, who diagnosed Stella with pyometritis, a deadly infection of her reproductive organs. Stella had apparently been over-bred until her uterus gave out, and then her owner had dumped her. The vet recommended surgery, and Beth was getting ready to leave town, so she did the best thing she could—she called our rescue. We took Stella in and gave her love, attention, and safety, which turned out to be all she needed. After two weeks Beth adopted Stella, and she has been on the mend ever since! *-Angie Persch*

Scared Straight: Men, vacuum cleaners, and dishes clanking (among many other things) used to send Subi into paroxysms of fear and shaking. We worked patiently on getting her used to noises and met at least one stranger a day, until months of how-do-you-do's paid off. Subi's now so comfortable that she's become a therapy dog, giving those in need the "Subi brand" of unconditional love. *-Lakshme Someswaran*

The Picky Eater: When I rescued Corey he was about 10 months old and all skin and bones. Food was a battle; after about a month of eating a decent dog food, Corey stopped eating and started losing weight. I tried adding canned food, which only worked for about a week. We then tried many different foods, but it wasn't until we cut out chicken and grains that Corey really thrived. It turns out dogs can be allergic to proteins and/or grains, and we were able to find a grain-free, chicken-free brand Corey really liked. *- Beth Carey*

Horror Movie: Betty Lou had been shot multiple times. Maggots had infested her wounds and were devouring her skin. She was also horribly malnourished and dirty. One vet had thought to euthanize her, but our vet instead gave her daily baths to exfoliate her dead skin and drown the maggots, good food, and antibiotics. Betty amazed everyone with the speed of her recovery, and her sweet, loving personality came shining through! *-Lee Mitchell*

"Horrible Case of Mange" Was an Understatement: When I met Nemo, I couldn't tell if he was fawn or brindle (turns out he's fawn), he had no hair, scabs covered his entire body, and not one bit of sparkle was left in his beautiful, brown eyes. As rescuers we weren't sure if there was anything we could do, but we just kept thinking "this is only demodex mange." It was a long, slow process, but antibiotics and daily doses of ivermectin eventually returned the sparkle to his eyes (and the fur to his skin). *-Kristy Gard*

Love Comes Back

Legacy Boxer Rescue received a standing ovation when I picked up Echo. The Longview Shelter workers loved Echo *very* much, and they were thrilled she had made it into rescue because it meant a chance for her to find a good home.

Echo lived with me as a foster and in time was placed with the perfect family. She never looked back, which always seems to be the case. When the right home is found, no matter how much love the dogs have for me, they never look back as they leave with their new guardians.

I'm the one left driving home with tears in my eyes, as the dogs look towards their new futures. For the most part, this is the hardest part of rescue, even when I know it is best for them and for me. After all, with each dog adopted I'm open to save another. No matter—I'm still going to fall in love with them all.

A Poem for Echo

Standing on a mountaintop and yelling in the wind,
You've heard your voice come back to you again, again, again.

The echo of the words you shout resounds throughout the trees,
And all who care to listen hear your words upon the breeze.

I had no voice with which to cry, so Angels spread their wings,
Out of love they shed their tears and started pulling heartstrings.

Days, they came and went, and soon the bridge I'd have to cross,
No one had the room for me, would anyone feel my loss?

In sad silence I sat waiting—the end was drawing near,
I gave up hope until I heard, "Legacy is here!"

It looks like all the Angels kept putting out the plea,
They never gave up hope there'd be a foster home for me.

Now my name is Echo and I've seen the mountaintop,
Where a hundred earthly Angels sing, their voices never stop.

If you open up your heart and listen carefully,
In the silence my voice echoes, "Love eternally."

 *Kathy A. Becton*

About Happy Tails Books™

Happy Tails Books™ was created to help support animal rescue efforts by showcasing the love, happiness, and joy adopted dogs have to offer. With the help of animal rescue groups, stories are submitted by people who have adopted dogs, and then Happy Tails Books™ compiles them into breed-specific books. These books serve not only to entertain, but also to educate readers about dog adoption and the characteristics of each specific type of dog. Happy Tails Books™ donates a significant portion of proceeds back to the rescue groups who help gather stories for the books.

 Happy Tails Books™

To submit a story or learn about other books Happy Tails Books™ publishes, please visit our website at http://happytailsbooks.com.

We're Writing Books about
Your Favorite Dogs!

Schnauzer   Chihuahua   Golden Retriever   PUG

DACHSHUND   German Shepherd   Collie   Boxer

Labrador Retriever   Husky   Beagle   ALL AMERICAN

Border Collie   Pit Bull Terrier   Shih Tzu   Miniature Pinscher

Chow Chow   Australian Shepherd   Rottweiler   Greyhound

Boston Terrier   Jack Russell   Poodle   Cocker Spaniel

GREAT DANE   Doberman Pinscher   Yorkie   SHEEPDOG

ST. BERNARD   Pointer   Blue Heeler

Find Them at Happytailsbooks.com!

Make your dog famous!

Do you have a great story about your adopted dog? We are looking for stories, poems, and even your dog's favorite recipes to include on our website and in upcoming books! Please visit the website below for story guidelines and submission instructions. **http://happytailsbooks.com/ submit.htm**